BRAD & JEN

*The Rise and Fall of
Hollywood's Golden Couple*

Wenner Media

BRAD & JEN

*The Rise and Fall of
Hollywood's Golden Couple*

By Mara Reinstein and
Joey Bartolomeo

Wenner Media
New York

BRAD & JEN: *The Rise and Fall of Hollywood's Golden Couple*

A Wenner Books Book
Wenner Books paperback/February 2005

Wenner Books
1290 Avenue of the Americas
2nd Floor
NY, NY 10104

A LifeTime Media Production
LifeTime Media, Inc.
352 Seventh Avenue, 15th Floor
New York, NY 10001
www.lifetimemedia.com

ISBN 1-932958-57-6

Published simultaneously in the United States and Canada.

PRINTED IN THE UNITED STATES OF AMERICA

10 9 8 7 6 5 4 3 2 1

Acknowledgments

Our thanks go to everyone at Wenner Books, our enthusiastic editor Nick Maier, everyone at LifeTime Media, and *Us Weekly* editor-in-chief Janice Min, who told us we knew so much about Brad and Jen that we could write this book in our sleep. We also couldn't have done it without the help and support of Andrew Sroka, David Guggenheim, Andrew Goulet, and Shelley Reinstein. We would also like to acknowledge the hard-working staff of *Us Weekly*, who have tirelessly covered the Golden Couple over the years. Thanks also to Lucy Danziger, Uncle Kenny, and their pals for their insight; Mike Steele (the voice of reason); Gina Way and the cast of *Fat Pig* for providing the light at the end of the tunnel; and, of course, our friends and families who were understanding, encouraging, and still loved us at our crankiest moments.

Contents

CHAPTER 1

The Split Heard 'Round the World

"We would like to announce that after seven years together we have decided to formally separate. For those who follow these sorts of things, we would like to explain that our separation is not the result of any of the speculations reported by the tabloid media. This decision is the result of much thoughtful consideration. We happily remain committed and caring friends with great love and admiration for one another. We ask in advance for your kindness and sensitivity in the coming months."

—*Respectfully, Jennifer Aniston & Brad Pitt*

In the world of celebrity watching it's the day that will live in infamy: On January 7, 2005, Jennifer Aniston and Brad Pitt shocked the world by announcing that four and a half years after their storybook wedding, they had decided to split up.

Stephen Huvane, Aniston's spokesperson, said, "The statement speaks for itself," a heart-felt-yet-cryptic explanation that did little to comfort grieving fans. After all, ever since the stylish *Friends* superstar and the sexy, Midwestern heartthrob were spotted together at a 1998 concert and then tied the knot with a $1 million ceremony on July 29, 2000, they were considered the closest thing Hollywood had to a royal couple — with the breathless tabloid headlines and the tawdry rumors to prove it.

Indeed, the Pitts seemed to have it all: The glamour, the career clout, the sun-kissed good looks, and, perhaps most importantly, the love. "It's a real gift when you find someone to share your life with," Aniston told *Redbook* in 2001. Her husband reiterated the same sentiment three years later in *Vanity Fair*. "Just when you think you've gotten all you can out of it, you get knocked upside the head," he said. "It's good fun. We still have that friendship; we still have a good laugh." And every time they glowed about their union, gazed at each other on the red carpet, and spoke of their desire to have a family, their aura only seemed to grow. This was not another Bennifer, Britney and Justin, or Tom and Nicole. If anyone could withstand the glare and pressure of a relationship in the spotlight, the Golden Couple could.

Even as the rumors of trouble surfaced, the couple sent out mixed signals about the relationship until the bitter end. Pitt spent his forty-first birthday in Los Angeles while his wife was across the Atlantic in London. There were reports that when she arrived at LAX airport, she was not wearing her wedding ring. Yet, before fans could blink, the couple enjoyed a luxurious and relaxing eight-day New Year's vacation with best pals Courteney Cox and David Arquette (and their seven-month-old daughter Coco) in the exotic Caribbean island of Anguilla. Twenty-four hours before they went public with the breakup, Brad and Jennifer were photographed kissing each other (three times!) during a leisurely stroll on the beach. "They looked so lovey," one eyewitness said. "They were clearly infatuated with each other. It was as if no one else was on the beach."

The Anguilla locals weren't the only ones baffled by the split. "It is really sad, I feel bad for them," Beth Katz, the *Friends'* makeup artist, added. Said another pal, "It was actually a surprise. They were discussing this only between themselves."

Surely, the pair's friends, coworkers, and publicists had been extremely protective of the relationship. Just before Christmas 2004, Aniston's rep announced, "There is no split. They are fine. Those stories [of trouble] are totally false." It was that kind of closed-ranks mentality around the guarded couple that helps explain why the relationship's deterioration remained one of Hollywood's best-kept secrets.

But it didn't take long for friends and associates to elaborate on the reasons behind the breakup once the damn broke open. It turned out the seemingly idyllic relationship had been so strained for so long that, according to an insider, Pitt's month long, worldwide publicity blitz for his caper *Ocean's Twelve* in December 2004 was actually a trial separation period.

The most common explanation for the marital strife was the baby factor. In teary-eyed interviews, Aniston and Pitt had publicly expressed a desire for kids — ranging from his seven to her two. "I was born with the hips to make babies... You can have the baby on one arm and the script on another," Aniston said in early 2004. Pitt seconded the motion during an interview with Oprah Winfrey a few months later: "I'm really looking forward to it. I finally feel like I've got my stuff together where I'm ready for that." But the couple's only joint project during their union was their production company, Plan B.

As one source explained it bluntly, "Brad wanted a family from the time they got married [but] Jen was the one who wanted to wait."

Indeed, in hopes of branching out of Rachel Green, her flighty *Friends* alter-ego of ten years, Aniston took on a whopping six movie projects almost immediately after the hit sitcom wrapped production in January 2004. That summer, she filmed the comedy *Rumor Has It*, in which she played a woman who learns her grandmother was possibly the inspiration for *The Graduate*'s Mrs. Robinson. By the year's end, she spent time in Chicago and London working on the thriller *Derailed* opposite sexy Brit Clive Owen. At the start of 2005, Aniston began work on the comedy *Friends with Money*. The plethora of projects seemed curious at best, especially since Aniston had previously told *InStyle*, "I'm seeing the bigger picture, realizing that family and enjoying your life are more important than the next role."

Meanwhile, Pitt — a bona fide superstar for a decade — has been pursuing his sizeable extracurricular activities outside show business. In the past twelve months, the die-hard Democrat spoke at his alma mater, the University of Missouri-Columbia, to campaign for presidential candidate John Kerry. A month later, he was named a special ambassador in Nelson Mandela's fight against AIDS and met with children at a Johannesburg, South Africa orphanage. "Brad thinks of movies as important, but he has the mindset of 'been there, done that,'" explained a source. "She's more career-driven."

But in the end, differences likely led to the couple's demise. Aniston has admitted her favorite activity is staying home and reading a good book while Pitt spent more and more time carousing until the wee hours with *Ocean's Twelve* cast mate George Clooney and nightclub impresario Rande Gerber. "It was obvious to everyone that he felt like a caged animal when he was with Jen," an Aniston pal revealed. "And he felt more free when she wasn't around."

Then there were the contrasting backgrounds: She was a child of divorce who's been estranged from mom, Nancy, since 1999; he grew up in a small Missouri city with a wholesome, close-knit family. "It bothered Brad that Jennifer wasn't close to her family," said a source close to the couple. "She's more about her friends; he's more about family."

Still, Aniston has always seemed determined to create her own sense of family, no matter her struggles, and still expressed a desire to rise above her past and to make a new life for herself and her husband throughout 2004.

Sadly, a lot can change in a year.

CHAPTER 2

The Ex Factor

Looking back at Aniston and Pitt's respective relationship histories, it's a small wonder they even made it to the second date.

The daughter of Nancy, an actress and model, and John, also an actor best known for his role as *Days of Our Lives*' evil Victor Kiriakis, Aniston grew up in Sherman Oaks, California, and Greece, before her family settled in New York City (along with half-brother John Melnick, from Nancy's previous marriage). At the age of nine the future actress came home from a party to find her father gone. At age twelve, she once recalled, she was sent to her room for "not being interesting enough." Her mother also chided her for having full cheeks and a skinny nose. She still admits that, as a result of her childhood and adolescence, she was constantly insecure and worrisome as an adult. (Aniston has credited Pitt with the turnaround: "I know it's said you should love yourself before you can be in a relationship, but, hell, I did it backward. I fell in love with myself as he fell in love with me," she said in

O, *The Oprah Magazine*.)

The divorce, naturally, impacted Aniston and her subsequent relationships. "I have always been somebody that really wants to be married," she said in 1997 while promoting her film (and future flop) *Picture Perfect*. "And I don't know if that's just so I can do it differently than my parents did and prove that marriage does work." Later in the same interview, she also said, "I'm cautious about getting married. My parents' divorce makes me very aware of what to look for in a partner and who to trust."

In her early twenties, Aniston put that trust in fellow actors. She briefly dated Charlie Schlatter, her costar in the short-lived 1990 NBC TV version of *Ferris Bueller*, but when the series fell apart, so did their relationship. In the early nineties, Aniston also dated little-known thespian Daniel MacDonald, but called it quits shortly before she was cast in *Friends* in 1994. Her first beau, once she joined her fictional New York City roommates on the now legendary sitcom, was the dread-locked Counting Crows singer Adam Duritz, whom she briefly dated in 1995.

Just around the time Aniston's character, Rachel, memorably kissed Ross Geller for the first time on the doorstep of Central Perk in *Friends*, the young actress was set up with actor Tate Donovan. In 1997, she recalled her first date: "He said we were going to dinner and I got my hair done. I put on this major dress. Then he took me to a strip mall food court. Later, Tate told me he did it to see if I was one of those stuck-up girls."

Donovan was so spooked by the paparazzi on their dates that he and Aniston broke things off after only a month. Three months later he was back and the couple exchanged Irish Claddagh rings as a symbol of their love on their first anniversary together. On Valentine's Day in 1997, Donovan surprised his sweetheart by placing a nine-week-old Australian sheep dog, named Enzo, in her *Friends* dressing room. During the summer, she showed up on his arm for the big New York City premiere of *Hercules*. Mixing work with pleasure, she also guest-starred on his fledgling Fox sitcom, *Partners*, in 1996. "He's a nice guy — a good guy," Aniston said at the time. "I reached that point [where] I'm not going to deal with the bastards anymore."

But by the time Aniston arranged for Donovan to play her love interest on the fourth season of *Friends* in 1998 (two and a half years into the relationship), their days were numbered. "We were fighting when I was on *Friends*," Donovan told a magazine in 2003. "We were already breaking up. Our split didn't happen suddenly. It was in the cards for a while. She likes top-notch hotels and luxury; I like B&Bs and riding my bike. That's the most shallow version of it, but it's indicative of our personalities."

Donovan, who also dated Sandra Bullock for nearly four years, went on to star in the Fox hit *The O.C.*, where he plays Jimmy Cooper, Mischa Barton's on-screen dad.

Aniston and Donovan broke up in April 1998. Five months later, she snagged a new beau. His name was Brad Pitt.

★ ★ ★

If it's true that opposites attract, Jennifer Aniston and Brad Pitt were made for each other.

The eldest child of Bill, a trucking company manager, and Jane, a high school counselor, Pitt grew up in the comfortable small city of Springfield, Missouri. He went on to attend the University of Missouri-at Columbia and was so charmingly popular in his Sigma Chi fraternity, girls practically lined up for dates. But in 1986, in what's become something of a Hollywood legend, the ambitious Pitt left school just two credits shy of an advertising journalism degree to drive out to Los Angeles in his Datsun and try his hand at acting. He had just $325 on him. "It was the realization that those things I wished were around that weren't around — I could go for," Pitt told *Vanity Fair* in 2004.

At first, the parts — which included guest-appearances in *Dallas* and *Growing Pains* — were small, but at least he got the chance to bond with his leading ladies. A role in the ABC sitcom *Head of the Class* in 1988 led to a brief relationship with Robin Givens, who had recently left a tumultuous relationship with boxer Mike Tyson. Givens told Oprah Winfrey in 2004 that after one romantic evening, Tyson knocked on Pitt's door demanding to talk to his estranged wife.

After dating Jill Schoelen (an actress whom he met on the slasher pic *Cutting Class*) in 1989, Pitt became taken with young Juliette Lewis, his costar in the 1990 TV movie *Too Young to Die?* The two dated for three years as each went through a critical arc in their respective careers. In 1991, he finally capitalized on his looks with his role as a charming hitch-hiker/thief who seduces Geena Davis in the female buddy movie *Thelma & Louise*. For her star turn, Lewis played a rebellious teen seduced by Robert De Niro in the thriller *Cape Fear* which earned her an Oscar nomination for Best Supporting Actress. As the two saw their stars rise in the early nineties, they decided to play a dysfunctional couple in the dark thriller, 1993's *Kalifornia*. They split shortly after the film was released (and subsequently died at the box office).

Pitt met Gwyneth Paltrow casually through friends in 1994. At that point, the twenty-two-year-old willowy beauty was known as much for her family pedigree (Gwyn is the daughter of Bruce Paltrow, the *St. Elsewhere* producer, and actress Blythe Danner) as her acting chops. Pitt, meanwhile, was about to kick-start his heartthrob status into overdrive with the one-two punch of *Interview with the Vampire* and *Legends of the Fall*. But the sparks didn't fly until months later, when the two costarred in the grisly thriller *Seven* (Paltrow played Pitt's doomed wife). "I started getting a crush on him," she told the Los Angeles Times in 1996. "I'm like 'Are you sane? You can't get a crush on Brad Pitt. Get hold of yourself.'" Pitt, on the other hand, didn't hold back. When he won the Golden Globe for his performance in

12 Monkeys in January 1996, he thanked Paltrow as "my angel."

Despite the east-coast upper-crust vs. Midwestern middle-class roots, the two looked positively blissful together as they hit locales as varied as the White House and NYC biker bar Hogs & Heffers. As reported in a magazine at the time, the couple also enjoyed mellow nights together at home playing games, watching TV, and dining with pals. They also pledged to never spend more than two weeks apart, despite their hectic schedules. "Brad's the one good one, and I got him," Paltrow was quoted as saying.

Pitt finally popped the question with a ring — a band with four diamonds — in December 1996 in Argentina, where he was filming the historical drama *Seven Years in Tibet*. Weeks later, Pitt brought her to Springfield to meet his parents. They reportedly celebrated the announcement by dining at the not-so-chic restaurant Red Lobster. "I can't wait for the wedding, man," he told *Rolling Stone*. "Walk down the aisle, wear the ring, kiss the bride. Oh, it's going to be great."

Pitt, however, suddenly broke off the engagement in June 1997. "It's not because of any one specific event," his publicist told the press. Of course, almost immediately, tongues were wagging. Sources close to the couple denied any infidelity, though many pointed out Pitt's fears of commitment and hesitation about getting involved with the frenzy of a wedding. (One report had the actor night-crawling in New York City just four days after the announcement, looking happy.) Although the end of the Paltrow and Pitt union came suddenly and unexpectedly, one factor may have weighed on any developing tensions between the couple — a set of *Penthouse* photos of Pitt and Paltrow frolicking in the nude. Pitt filed a lawsuit, and the risqué issue was recalled. To this day, neither Pitt nor Paltrow has publicly discussed the reason behind the breakup.

In hindsight, of course, it should be noted that Paltrow admitted she'd be willing to put children ahead of a white-hot career: "I love acting," she said, "but it's not the most important thing."

Fast forward to May of 2004: Paltrow and husband of seven months, Coldplay singer Chris Martin, welcomed the birth of daughter Apple Blythe Allison Martin.

CHAPTER 3

How They Fell in Love

For Jennifer Aniston and Brad Pitt, the close-knit community of Hollywood worked in their favor. Indeed, the two first met way back in 1994 during a casual get-together. "He was just this sweet guy from Missouri, you know?" she told *Rolling Stone* in 2001. "A normal guy." Both were involved in serious relationships at the time, she with Donovan and he with Paltrow. Although Aniston had said, "It was not the right time," the spark was there. The two couples often ended up at the same parties and hung out together.

When they went back to living the single life, their managers sensed the time was right for a match-up. Pitt called Aniston just before she left for London to film a *Friends* episode in the spring of 1998, asking if he could help her pack and bring her coffee. "I was so nervous that I never called him back," Aniston admitted to Oprah Winfrey. "I pretended I got the message too late. When I got back from England, we had a date."

The two hung out that first evening at his

Los Feliz, California, bachelor pad and just like that, a Hollywood couple was born. "Yes, I fell in love on our first date," Aniston told *O*. Later, reminiscing with Diane Sawyer, she said, "We both knew [right away]… it was weird." She added that she thought, "That was a really easy evening. That was really fun."

For months, Pitt and Aniston kept their relationship on the DL, as they usually spent their nights indoors watching TV, eating Mexican food, and playing poker (in a stroke of good luck, neither one at the time had to do the PR rounds to promote any new projects). Their private romance, however, became an open secret when they were photographed nuzzling backstage at the Washington D.C. Tibetan Freedom Concert in the summer of 1998. That photo was reprinted around the world, much to the glee of their worshipful fans. Aniston's reaction? "Oy! You just think, 'Here we go.'"

Nevertheless, the new couple moved at their own pace. In November 1998, for the NYC premiere of Pitt's big-budget dramedy *Meet Joe Black*, the two went to extraordinary means to deny their relationship. They holed up all day in a suite at the Four Seasons Hotel, waiting for the arrival of their handlers and presidential-level security. A limo picked them up, and the actors' performances began. First, Pitt walked the red carpet by himself, ignoring the "where's Jennifer?" shouts from the press. Aniston, meanwhile, escorted by her agent, snuck in through a back entrance. Things were only slightly less controlled at the invitation-only after-party at the Metropolitan Club: Pitt had told his handlers to keep the press away from the party, but some enterprising reporters still managed to get in and witness the couple's romantic reunion — which included a hug and kiss — at Pitt's table.

By 1999, the relationship was full speed ahead. On February 6, Pitt threw Aniston a thirtieth birthday party at L.A. hotspot restaurant Barfly. Less than a week later, the pair flew a group of nine friends on a chartered private jet to Acapulco for a luxurious weekend to celebrate Aniston's big day and Valentine's Day. On February 14, with fireworks exploding over the Pacific coast, Pitt and Aniston danced and snuggled until five in the morning. When *Friends* wrapped for the season that spring, Pitt had already become a constant on-set visitor, and the couple traveled to Europe, where they stayed at the Alhambra palace in Granada, Spain. In perhaps a nod to Rachel and Ross's quickie Las Vegas wedding in the *Friends* fifth season finale in May 1999, they registered in hotels as "Mr. and Mrs. Ross Vegas."

Stateside, the couple spent their courtship driving up the Malibu coast and through the Sierra Nevada mountain range listening to Aniston's favorite musician, the late singer-songwriter Jeff Buckley. The self-described homebodies also regularly hung out with pals like costar Matt LeBlanc and his then-fiancée, Melissa McKnight, at either Aniston's two-bedroom Hollywood Hills bungalow or Pitt's place. "Jennifer's a lot more peaceful now, like a woman who's in a good relationship," Aniston's sitcom costar Lisa Kudrow said in 1999. "There's not a lot to say about them because there are no problems. They're both light-years ahead of themselves. You know how your grandparents have a certain perspective about life? They've got that now."

Ever the supportive couple, Aniston shaved Pitt's head before he filmed his part as charismatic psychopath Tyler Durden in the cutting-edge drama *Fight Club*. They attended the romantic nuptials of Courteney Cox and David Arquette on June 12 in San Francisco. In September, he escorted her to the Emmy

Awards — their first official outing as a couple.

Then the ultimate sign of faith in their relationship: The press-shy couple opened up about each other to the media. For one interview and photo shoot, Aniston went so far as to *not* hide the two photos of Pitt on display in her home. "I'm not withholding, just preserving something that's mine," Aniston told *Rolling Stone*. "To talk about a relationship trivializes something that's nobody's business." Pressed to say something about Brad, she added, "I'll just tell you that this is the happiest time of my life. I'm not saying why, it's for a lot of reasons: work, love, family, just life — all of it."

Of course, the relationship was not without its outside obstacles. In 1996, Nancy Aniston had gossiped about her daughter's struggles on a talk show. By the time Mom published the tell-all *From Mother and Daughter to Friends: A Memoir*, Aniston estranged herself from the relationship. "My mother didn't know where she ended and began," Aniston later said in *Vanity Fair*. "This separation needed to happen for both of us… To feel that someone is trying to live through me… It's a tough one."

Pitt received the scare of his life in early 1999 when an overzealous young female fan broke into his home and went to sleep. His big screen career was equally frightful: Three consecutive starring vehicles, *Seven Years in Tibet*, *The Devil's Own*, and *Meet Joe Black* all failed miserably at the box office.

The troubles, he said, "weren't any worse than anyone else's. I walked into a couple of traps, into the minefields, that's all... And I'll step in a few more."

☆ ☆ ☆

Despite their history with broken hearts, that magic moment came when Pitt proposed to Aniston in early 1999 — after just five months of dating. He helped design the diamond engagement ring himself with Italian jeweler, Damiani. "I didn't want to commit to it," Pitt was quoted as saying. "I thought marriage was just a piece of paper, but Jen showed me better, and she was right. I saw the light."

To celebrate the upcoming nuptials, Pitt organized a surprise Moroccan-themed party for his future wife in L.A. "Brad called me to arrange it," said party planner Chris Breed. "He took control over the arrangements because he wanted it to be really special for her. He wanted a Moroccan theme and was very specific about the romantic atmosphere we were going to create. It was really important to him that he make the party as perfect as possible for her... He was obviously very in love and wanted to do whatever he could to make Jen happy."

The pair never officially announced their engagement. Perhaps that's why fans were so shocked when, during a Sting concert in New York City on November 21, 1999, the couple suddenly emerged onstage and showed off her sparkler. One magazine reported, "The crowd went nuts." And with good reason: They then sang along to the hit, "Fill Her Up."

We're going to Vegas
We're gonna get wed

Amazingly, the couple's reps denied that Aniston flashed an engagement ring even when she confirmed the engagement to onlookers at the concert's private after-party!

The adoring public, however, knew. Indeed, the first big celebrity wedding of the new century was just months away.

CHAPTER 4

The Big Day

The perfect couple went ahead with planning their perfect $1 million wedding, to be held on July 29, 2000.

"We were engaged for about a year and a half and we just got married when it felt right," said Pitt. For Aniston (and her close circle of girlfriends) organizing the nuptials meant making peace with the idea that she'd found a Mr. Right in Mr. Pitt. "My friends were all supportive," she said in 2001. "Especially when they found out what a loving human being Brad is. He just disarms you immediately. But, I mean, nobody went, 'Dude. Brad Pitt!' And gave me a thumbs up and a wink. They were just happy for me."

Aniston's pre-wedding agenda was as common as any other bride-to-be's. Step one: Get in shape. The actress, who famously shed thirty pounds (she later claimed it was ten) at her agent's behest to land the role of Rachel Green in 1994, took up a strict new workout regimen of cardio and weightlifting to tone up her arms and used the low-carb "Zone" diet to manage her weight.

Step two: Find a gown. Of course, nothing off-the-rack would do for a Hollywood superstar, so she commissioned former Prada designer Lawrence Steele to create something special. The dress, which the public glimpsed in a single black-and-white picture released to the media, featured beading, a high, halter neck, and an open back. (The groom looked sleek in a four-button black tux by Paris designer Hedi Slimane.) She topped it off, according to one magazine, with a pearl-and-Swarovski crystal crown.

Step three: Nail down the details. The bridal party included Pitt's father, Bill, and brother Doug (who wore Prada), and Aniston's longtime best friends Kristin Hahn and Andrea Bendewald (who were lucky enough to wear green slip dresses designed by Steele). For the location, the couple settled on TV producer Marcy Carsey's five-acre Malibu estate overlooking the Pacific ocean. They hired Beverly Hills florist La Premiere to take care of the arrangements (which were said to include roses, tulips, and wisteria), and Rosebud bakery to whip up the cake. (The six-tier confection was assembled at the wedding location, it was said.)

Marc Friedland of Creative Intelligence Inc. handled the invitations for the 200 guests. First came phone calls, said a report, then came the actual paper invite. Who made the cut? Old friends Melissa Etheridge (who was reported to have rocked the reception with a rendition of Led Zeppelin's "Whole Lotta Love"); Dermot Mulroney and Catherine Keener; *Friends* costars Matthew Perry, Courteney Cox (with husband David Arquette); David Schwimmer (who brought then-girlfriend actress Mili Avital); and Lisa Kudrow with husband Michel Stern. And, of course, celebrity pals and coworkers including Pitt's *Fight Club* costar Edward Norton with then-girlfriend Salma Hayek; Gwen Stefani and Gavin Rossdale; David Spade, Kathy Najimy, and Cameron Diaz.

"I had those typical jitters the day before my wedding," Aniston later admitted. "But the day of, I was just excited in a good way. The nice thing about a wedding now is it's not just a chick thing. It's a team effort. The stereotype used to be men grumbling like, 'Why are you making me do this?' " In fact, it was said that Pitt wanted the wedding to have a Japanese feel, so the couple requested a Zen garden-inspired fountain; lotus flowers were scattered in the water on the Big Day, as was reported by *People* magazine.

The actor was also responsible for contacting Mary Buckley, mother of the late singer-songwriter Jeff Buckley, to get permission to play her son's music at the wedding. "It became the soundtrack to their romance," said Mary in 2001. "Before their wedding, Brad asked to meet with me and he asked me if I would mind if he made a compilation of Jeff's music to play at the wedding. He said the music had special significance to him and Jen. He wanted it playing at the reception because it meant that much to them."

Additionally, the couple hired a gospel choir (which sang the old-time hit "Love Is the Greatest Thing" along with one of the couple's favorite songs by the rock band Blur), a string quartet, a six-piece band and Dakota Horvath, a 12-year-old Frank Sinatra-style crooner, who, it was said, Pitt had seen on stage years before. Plus, in a nod to Aniston's Greek heritage, a bouzouki band was hired for the reception.

And then there were the only-in-Hollywood details. Taking a page from the Tom Cruise and Nicole Kidman handbook, the pair required staffers to sign a confidentiality agreement making them liable for a penalty of up to $100,000 if they gabbed about the lavish ceremony. Concerned about paparazzi-filled helicopters crashing the party (as was the case when Madonna wed Sean Penn), it was also reported that they contacted the FAA and arranged to have a representative at the wedding. White tents, erected especially for the occasion, also helped prevent prying eyes. Nevertheless, the choppers began to swarm in advance of the nuptials. "Two days before the wedding, five helicopters were in the air. You couldn't talk to the person next to you," Doug Pitt, told a local Missouri paper.

As another security measure — which may have also prevented traffic jams — guests were not allowed to drive to Carsey's Malibu home. Instead, they parked at Malibu High School, where they were picked up and taken to the site in vans.

On July 29, the day of the wedding, Aniston's glam squad — hairstylist Chris McMillan and *Friends'* makeup artist, Robin Siegel — tended to the bride as the finishing touches were put on the property. According to one account, lanterns and imported brown sugar candles were distributed around the premises. Meanwhile, caterers from *Along Came Mary* tended to the hors d'oeuvres (reported to include caviar, gourmet pizza, and shrimp) and dinner (said to be risotto, pasta, lobster, crab, and peppercorn beef).

The magic began at 6:30 P.M., when a ring-bearer, flower girls (in white dresses and reportedly blowing bubbles and tossing petals), and the bridesmaids made their way down the linen-covered aisle. Finally, it was Aniston's turn. With her father, John, by her side — and four-inch high Manolo Blahnik shoes on her feet — Aniston strolled down the aisle.

The emotional fifteen-minute ceremony was the stuff fairytale movies — and funny *Friends*' wedding episodes — were made of. Early reports claimed that Doug dropped his brother's wedding ring during the ceremony. "It was a cute moment," said Doug, who added that the ring slipped out of his *dad's* hand during the exchange to his son. The creative couple wrote their own vows, which shed some light on the give-and-take of their relationship. Aniston promised to always make Pitt's "favorite banana milk shake." Pitt, meanwhile, pledged to "split the difference on the thermostat."

Getting through the rest of the ceremony, however, wasn't so easy. According to one account, the bride missed her cue when it was time to join Pitt in the vows. "I've never done this before!" she announced. Finally, after exchanging the Damiani white-gold wedding bands, they declared, "With this ring, I thee wed ... so that all the world may know my love for you."

One year later, Aniston remarked to *Rolling Stone*, "There is nothing more moving than seeing a man cry at his own wedding."

The night continued with a slide show featuring photos of the couple, dinner, dancing, and plenty of champagne. Love wasn't the only thing in the air, though. A fireworks show — produced by the same people who put together Macy's annual 4th of July show in NYC — eventually lit up the sky.

A few years later, Matthew Perry summed up the evening by proclaiming, "[Brad and Jen's wedding] was the most romantic [night] of my life." Pitt's brother Doug echoed, "I really enjoyed myself. Brad and Jennifer did a great job planning it, and it far exceeded anything I expected. It was an event."

The legal merger of two of Hollywood's best-looking and most beloved actors, of course, was the most ballyhooed event of the year. Immediately, knockoffs of Aniston's

Lawrence Steele gown turned up in shops; people couldn't get enough of the details; and the fact that the Pitts refused to sell their photographs to the magazines of the world or the British tabloids only heightened the hysteria. Dakota Horvath was even interviewed the next week on the *Today* show.

Exactly how magical was the night? Consider Pitt's interesting wedding anecdote when he visited *The Tonight Show with Jay Leno* on February 1, 2001: "The paparazzi and I had a big game going on. I started getting a little carried away with it and Jen had to smack me around, remember why we were there. And we wanted to do a thing outside and we wanted to write our own ceremony and we just kind of gave up on it all. And something happened. At the very last minute when the ceremony started, the press backed off and I really have to thank them. They were so cool with us. They let us have our moment. They let us have what turned out to be the highlight of my life. The night was amazing."

On October 25, 2000, Aniston made it official, breaking the hearts of Pitt-lovers around the world: She visited the Santa Monica Department of Motor Vehicles and registered her name as Jennifer Joanne Pitt. In an interview she recalled the first time she heard herself called by her married name — at the dentist's office. "I was there to have my wisdom teeth pulled ... The nurse opens the door and says, 'Mrs. Pitt?' I was like, 'Wow!'"

CHAPTER 5

The Honeymoon Period

Adjusting to domestic life isn't easy, even when you're the most famous wife in Hollywood and your husband is Brad Pitt.

Early in 2001, Aniston recounted the tough, emotionally unstable period after her July wedding and admitted to *Vanity Fair* that the stretch was one of the hardest of her life. She and Pitt faced family and work issues, fears, mistrust, and doubts. Still, the couple was resolute: they would get through the challenge. In 2000, in a fit of agitation, Aniston found temporary relief by chopping off her much-envied locks to a short bob. "I did it mainly to relieve me of the bondage of self," she explained. "It was the right time to do it — shed the skin — but I couldn't hate it more... I'm taking every horse vitamin there is to make it grow faster — blue-green algae, you name it."

There wasn't much time for moping, anyway. In November 2000 (just weeks after they beamed on the red carpet at the Emmy Awards), Pitt started filming the espionage thriller *Spy Game* with Robert Redford. It was the first time the couple spent a significant time apart, and prophetically, it wouldn't be the last. The production took him to England, Hungary, and Morocco. Just before Thanksgiving, Aniston, who had confessed she's deathly afraid of flying, boarded a plane to London and Budapest to visit her new husband. In turn, he jetted to Los Angeles from Morocco to spend his first married Christmas with his new wife.

The reunion was short lived. As soon as they rang in 2001 together, Pitt returned overseas to finish *Spy Game*. Aniston was resigned to attend the L.A. premiere of Pitt's indie caper *Snatch* on January 18 all by her lonesome. To ease the separation, the two used webcams, which allowed them to see each other via tiny cameras on their computers. "It rocks," he said. "You can't see movement really. It takes pictures every six seconds. But still, she gets to see what room I'm stuck in and I get to see her."

Almost as soon as Pitt finished filming *Spy Game*, he was off to Las Vegas to film the comic caper *Ocean's Eleven*, costarring fellow A-listers George Clooney, Matt Damon, and his love interest in the 2001 film *The Mexican*,

Julia Roberts. The schedule meant Pitt and Aniston had to miss their first Valentine's Day together as husband and wife. But Pitt had one heck of a plan B: As a surprise, he had Aniston's *Friends* dressing room decorated with 1,500 roses, and spelled out the words "I love my wife" with rose petals on the wall.

At least he was in town for Aniston's thirty-second birthday and did not disappoint. Pitt took her and forty guests to a bowling bash at the Hollywood Star Lanes, where he presented her with a sweatshirt, scented candle, and photo album. A few weeks later, they turned up arm-in-arm at the L.A. premiere of his comedy *The Mexican*. And during another early break from *Ocean's Eleven*, he returned to L.A. to take his bride to a Mexican lunch at Basix Café in West Hollywood. "The thing I was least prepared for was the pride I have whenever I look across at this woman," said Pitt.

Their love only intensified. One time, during the *Ocean's Eleven* production in spring of 2001, a producer knocked on Pitt's suite in the Bellagio Hotel to pick him up for a dinner with Clooney and Roberts. Pitt put him off and said, "I've got a date with my wife." He then closed the door and settled in for a romantic rendezvous with Aniston. As he explained to the producer, "*Friends* is coming on. I've got to watch her."

By March 2001, it was Aniston's turn to play the in-demand actress. Between her *Friends* shooting schedule, she decided to take a challenging new role in a film called *The Good Girl*. In the low-budget flick, Aniston had to de-glam herself to play a low-class, small-town grocery clerk who cheats on her husband with a troubled, much younger guy played by Jake Gyllenhaal. No designer duds here — Aniston spent most of the film in over-alls and loose jeans.

While filming *The Good Girl*, "she flew to Las Vegas to see Brad where he was filming *Ocean's Eleven*," said a source on the set. "She'd finish the film at 11 P.M. and then race off to see him for her one day off. And she was shooting *Friends* at the same time, so worked twenty-two days straight. She was incredibly devoted to the movie and to Brad and to the TV show. A real class act."

Pitt, too, visited Aniston on *The Good Girl* set and was rumored to have her trailer filled with flowers. He also joined her for the film's wrap party in late May at Guy's, a bar on Beverly Boulevard, where they partied with the cast and crew as a DJ played music well into the night. Partiers described the couple as the honeymooners they were, holding hands and cooing on the back patio. "They were very lovey-dovey," said one reveler. "Brad was real cool in black leather and Jennifer looked great." Although the mood of the party was mellow, Pitt was enthused as he approached a few stragglers at the end of the night and gushed about the venue. "It's really great for us to be here tonight," he said, "because this is the club where Jennifer and I first met."

In fact, the twosome was so gleefully in love, many speculated children were on the immediate agenda. The buzz certainly reached a fever pitch when, during a cliffhanger season finale of *Friends* in May 2001, it was revealed that Rachel Green was pregnant by a mystery father. Aniston later admitted that she and Pitt had "a window" to have a baby during the pregnant-Rachel storyline, but they obviously never capitalized on it. Instead, she denied to all that she was expecting. "I found it hysterical," she said of the persistent rumors. "I didn't get mad — I got a lot of free desserts."

Meanwhile, Pitt finished *Ocean's Eleven* in early June, which left time for the pair to spend their summer together. They started it off cheering on the L.A. Lakers against the Philadelphia 76ers at a game at the Staples Center. A few weeks later, the couple traveled to Milan, Italy, for a romantic weekend. On June 28, a chic-looking Aniston took Pitt and Clooney to the Giorgio Armani fashion show. As the designer unveiled his summer 2002 menswear collection, onlookers caught an even better show in the front row: Aniston had her arm nestled on Pitt's left thigh. The couple also reportedly renewed their wedding vows at Armani's home.

In early September 2001, as Aniston played a supportive girlfriend in the drama *Rock Star* with Mark Wahlberg, she grew more and more comfortable in her role as Mrs. Pitt. "You know if there's ever an argument, it's not like you can go 'screw you, I'm outta here!'" she said. "You're there. It's a beautiful thing to actually realize... It takes the heat and the weight off of things." Later, she waxed: "There's something about his spirit and soul and his gentleness and his kindness. He's one of the kindest people that I know" — not to mention "the sweetest goofball on the planet."

Her *Rock Star* screenwriter, John Stockwell, was even more in awe: "He's always aware, never talking across her, just always making sure she's comfortable, she's well fed and hydrated. He was like, 'Do you believe how hot she is? Can you believe she likes me?' Literally, his eyes do no wandering when he's with her. There can be girls flashing, dropping their tops and he doesn't seem to notice when she's around."

The couple's first full year of marriage was capped by a small-screen part with big-time buzz: A cameo on the *Friends'* Thanksgiving episode. For his must-see TV debut, Pitt played a formerly chubby high school class-mate of Rachel and Ross who despised Rachel so much back in the day that he started a ru-mor she was a hermaphrodite. "He was so ner-vous," Aniston later recalled on *The Oprah Winfrey Show*. "And he kept saying, 'I'm going to mess up my line. I'm going to mess up my first line,' and we were like, 'No, you're not go-ing to mess up your first line.' And he went through the door and we all looked at each other and we were like, 'He's going to mess up his first line,' and sure enough, he did. But he had to, I think."

By the time Pitt marked his thirty-eighth birthday in December, the couple had plenty to celebrate. For her husband's special day, Aniston fulfilled one of his longtime wishes.

Knowing that Pitt wanted to spend the night in a renowned Greene & Greene designed house on the cliffs of Northern California, Aniston sweet-talked the owners into handing over the keys for a romantic weekend.

Not surprisingly, the couple rang out 2001 in style as they traveled with best pals Courteney Cox and David Arquette to Cabo San Lucas, Mexico, where they frolicked in the luxurious Villas del Mar beach resort.

Cost?

An estimated $3,800 a night.

Happy New Year, indeed.

CHAPTER 6

Life as a Couple

Celebrities are known for having fabulous lives. They travel in private planes, stay in the most luxurious hotels, and can access anything money can buy. But they also like to stay in, get take-out, and play board games. In fact, that's how Pitt and Aniston spent much of their free time. "People think we have a life that's so glamorous," she said. "But it couldn't be more normal." She wasn't joking: "We get pizza and watch movies. We also play poker and look at design magazines. We're so boring," she said in O. Though the couple had professional obligations that forced them onto the red carpet regularly, they generally shunned the spotlight. "We are such homebodies," Aniston admitted. "We don't really go out. If a premiere comes up, we'll put on our fancy clothes and go, but those events are generally avoided at all costs."

Aniston, who hates that stars are made out to be virtual deities, has always made an effort to sell herself as the average person. "I work from 9 to 5 just like anyone else," she's said.

And like so many working women, when she gets home, she would not always cook dinner. "We're order-in freaks," she revealed. That said, when Pitt's family would visit the couple's Santa Barbara beach house, Aniston was known to barbeque and make homemade salsa. She also loved to make post-Thanksgiving sandwiches filled with turkey, mayo, and stuffing. And in 2004, she admitted she was trying to get handier in the kitchen. "I made pizza a couple weeks ago from scratch," she told a magazine. "I had a kind of Lucy-Ethel moment, flour all over me."

But both Pitt and Aniston loved going to restaurants, too. In fact, they used the outings to connect with friends and family — even each other. "We'll all go to dinner," her father, John Aniston, has said, "just walk in someplace, and it's not a big deal." Some of their favorite Italian spots include Il Sole, Balboa, and Orso, all in West Hollywood. When they craved Japanese food, the couple would hit West Hollywood hotspots Sushi Roku, Koi, or Hama Saku in West Los Angeles, where they liked to go for dinner-for-two. "Brad usually eats off her plate but she never eats off his," said a source, who added the stars were considered "a nice, friendly couple, and completely unpretentious."

The actress's favorite cuisine, however, is Mexican. Serve her corn chips, salsa, cheese, and guacamole, and she just can't get enough. "Really good Mexican food is hard to find, but I have my favorite places," she said. On weekends, it was not uncommon to find her with pals at Marix, a no-frills Tex-Mex cantina in West Hollywood. "Sunday's the day when the girls come over, we order in, or we go get Mexican and come back to the house and play Password or $25,000 Pyramid," explained Aniston in O. According to one Marix employee, "She comes in all the time. Usually she sits with a group of girlfriends and nobody really bothers her. Most of the time, people don't even realize she's here." Aniston usually sits at a corner table on the outdoor patio, where smoking is allowed. "She's always so nice to everyone," a bartender said, adding her drink of choice is a Patron margarita.

One trip to Marix in January 2003 sparked a touch of controversy. That night, her *Friends* costar David Schwimmer was opening in a play just around the corner. But instead of attending the performance with other cast mates and stars, Aniston was dining on the patio with three girlfriends. At around 10:30 P.M., she asked the waiter to have her car brought around. "I have to leave before everyone comes out of the theatre," she said. "I have to go now." Before she left, she plunked down Pitt's credit card. "It's on the husband," she said.

In London, one of their favorite haunts was Fifteen, chef Jamie Oliver's upscale London trattoria, which serves nouveau British cuisine. The couple got to know Oliver when Aniston flew him to Los Angeles to prepare a special surprise birthday meal for Pitt's birthday in 2003. "I was Brad's birthday gift!" the chef, who called the couple "great people," said. "We kept in touch." While in London on June 18, 2004, the pair dined at Fifteen with six friends, including model Claudia Schiffer, whose husband, Matthew Vaughn, produced *Snatch*, which starred Pitt. "It was lovely having them in," said Oliver. Aniston returned the compliment, "The food was delicious. It's a shame we're always so far away!"

At least they could check out his *Naked Chef* series on the Food Network. Watching the tube, in fact, was a favorite activity. *Friends*, of course, was a favorite. "Brad's always been a big fan of the show," Aniston said. "He was slightly like a stalker! He also loves *Will & Grace*. And he's addicted to *Survivor*.

He has to TiVo *Survivor* if *Friends* is on." Some of their Hollywood peers may pooh-pooh shows that don't feature fellow actors, but Aniston confessed she and her husband were drawn to them. "Our guilty pleasure is reality shows," she said. "We can't *not* watch."

When not camped out on the couch, the couple shared a love of music — "We do have similar tastes — very eclectic in that we'll listen to pretty much anything," Aniston said. Known to take in a concert now and then, there was the famous outing to the Tibetan Freedom Concert during their courtship, the Sting concert around the time of their engagement, and as a married couple in 2001, they took in the British band Bush at Los Angeles's Roxy nightclub. The following year, Aerosmith fan Aniston presented the legendary rockers with an MTV Icon award.

When it comes to finding peace of mind, Aniston heads for the hills. Hiking, she revealed, "really does sort of save me." And she and Pitt both indulge their creative sides. "I used to do a lot more painting and sculpting when I was younger and not working so much," she said in 2001. (After they had moved to Beverly Hills, Pitt converted Aniston's former Hollywood Hills home into an office and art studio.) She added, "I started really young, probably in grade school, and continued through my adulthood." The actor, who is passionate about architecture and aesthetics, even got into jewelry design. After co-creating Aniston's engagement ring and their wedding bands, he struck a formal deal with Damiani to co-design a line of jewelry, D.Side. His wife, he said, was his "inspiration."

Another passion of both stars was politics. In 2004, when Pitt wasn't working, he campaigned for Democratic presidential nominee John Kerry. On October 13, he and Aniston stepped out to a private screening and reception for the new film *Going Upriver: The Long War of John Kerry* and Pitt talked passionately to other guests about getting out the vote. A week later, he was at the University of Missouri-Columbia, his alma mater, where he campaigned for Kerry. His trip shocked many locals, including a manager at the Columbia Missourian newspaper. "We've offered and offered tons of times for him to come speak, and I can't believe it was this that finally brought him back!" revealed the source. Pitt's impending visit also sparked many coeds to get political. "All of the sudden, we had all these people that wanted to be part of the Young

Democrats!" said one student. "They were coming out of everywhere."

Even the actor himself was surprised by the turnout when he peeked through the curtains to check out the crowd of 1,500 students. (For the record, they were mostly women.) "I can't believe how many people are here!" he announced to everyone gathered backstage. When asked by one bystander if he thought taking a political stance was a risk for his career he responded, "Well, it's just a really important cause for me and I guess we'll find out later. But it's just very important to me."

When he finally took the stage, the auditorium became a madhouse. "The girls were screaming, going crazy, taking pictures and running to the front," reported an eyewitness. Pitt began his speech by reflecting on his days as an undergrad, but quickly moved on. "First of all, I'm not here to tell you who to vote for," he said, then muttered under his breath, "Vote for John Kerry." He explained to the audience why he supported the film, calling it "a work of art," touched on Kerry's political stance, and even cited the Declaration of Independence. "The first declaration says that all men are created equal, that they are all endowed with equal opportunities. Some would say that all

men are endowed." The crowd started screaming, and one girl yelled, "So are you!" Pitt
grinned. All kidding aside, Pitt's appearance
was effective. "It got people excited about the
election," said Caleb Lewis, president of the
university's chapter of Young Democrats.

Who would be elected president wasn't
Pitt's only concern leading up to the 2004
elections. Californians were also set to vote on
a proposition that would allocate money to
stem cell research, a highly controversial issue. In October, Pitt visited the *Today* show to
discuss the matter. "It's important that we
open up this field and we get them the funding
and the pathways they need to find these cures
that our scientists and our doctors believe are
there," he told Katie Couric. Pitt was not the
first Hollywood star to promote the research:
Michael J. Fox, who is afflicted with Parkin-
son's disease, and the late Christopher Reeve,
a quadriplegic, both appeared in ads to support funding.

Land mines have become another pet
cause of Pitt's. In November 2004, the actor
joined Nelson Mandela, Virgin empire billionaire Sir Richard Branson, and John Paul De-
Jorjia of Jon Paul Mitchell Systems in South
Africa, where they brought attention to the

Mineseekers charity, an organization raising money to build airships, which can detect underground landmines via satellite. "Brad wanted to use his celebrity to help make the world a better place to live," DeJorjia said after the trip. "Brad is not 'Hello, look at me! I'm doing this cause!' waving his flag around. He told me, 'For me to be involved, I want to know all about it. How do we make a difference?' His involvement is because he knows all about it and he likes what he hears. He asked me personally all about it. So he's very intelligent about [the cause]. Brad is a very good man." Or, as Pitt's *Fight Club* costar Helena Bonham Carter once said, "He's amazingly unspoiled by the stardom he's been burdened with."

Concerts, dinners, art, and politics? Despite Aniston's protests, it's clear the couple was not so boring after all.

CHAPTER 7

Their Friends

"I'll Be There For You" was the theme song to *Friends* (sung by the Rembrandts), but it could also describe Jennifer Aniston and Brad Pitt's relationships with their own tight-knit group of pals. As easy as it is for stars to drop friends as they ride up the ladder of fame, these two are known for remaining close to the people who knew them when. Even the relationships they've forged post-fame are genuine: "Courteney and Lisa, those are going to be the girls I'll know forever," Aniston once said of her former costars Cox and Kudrow.

Though Aniston remains close to all of her former costars, Cox and her husband seemed to have a special place in Aniston and Pitt's hearts: It was they who joined the Pitt's on their final trip to Anguilla before the breakup. When news of the split first leaked, sources were saying the couple had even invited Aniston to stay at their home until she figured out her next step. But that doesn't mean they were choosing sides. "Courteney and David will be there for *both* of them," said a source. "But they'll be closer to Jen — she and [Cox] have a strong bond." Indeed, Aniston has said of her friend, "She's been there for me in a lot of ways, and she's — really is the most dependable and loyal and funny as all get-out. I mean, she just cracks me up constantly."

Luckily, the husbands also got along. During the quartet's trip to Mexico in 2003, "It was boys with boys and girls with girls," a resort staffer said. Pitt and Arquette chartered a fishing boat (Pitt caught a 150-pound marlin; Arquette hooked two mahi-mahi), went snorkeling and ate lunch at the local Johnny Rockets (they ordered burgers and malts). The women preferred to take it easy by relaxing at their private pool (the couples shared a five-bedroom, $6,000-a-night beach house) while receiving house calls from a personal masseuse. However, at one point, the entire group was spotted tooling around by the beach on motorized scooters.

The relationship between Aniston and Cox was forged back in 1994 when they both auditioned for the NBC sitcom. (Cox was auditioning for the role of Rachel.) For Aniston, the attraction was nearly instant. "I remember meeting Courteney and I was enraptured," she said in *Vogue*. "First of all, that someone's face could be that beautiful? And it goes way beyond that. Her spirit is infectious. She's somebody you are around and you just want to be a better person. You want to live! She lives so fully."

Aniston looks up to Cox so much that she even took up the same fitness regimen. Despite her professed hatred for yoga, Aniston began practicing Budokon, a blend of yoga and martial arts designed to develop core strength and flexibility. The one thing Cox can't get her to do, though, is karaoke. "Courteney is the karaoke queen," Aniston said. "She just belts it out at the top of her lungs...Brad gets up there, but I don't. I sit in the back and get harassed by Courteney. She's relentless."

For her part, Cox has said she couldn't get enough of Aniston, even while they worked together. As she explained in a magazine in 2002, "Sometimes I can't believe that we'll spend the whole day at work and then, let's say, we get out of work a little early and there's time to go get something to eat — and we'll actually do that! I say, 'We should split up, go somewhere else, see some other people.' But we don't. It's pathetic, I know." Their bond is so strong that Aniston has even joked, "If we were lesbians we would marry each other."

Male fantasies aside, that doesn't seem

likely. But even Arquette said the women were "a great support system for each other." Before Cox gave birth to daughter Coco in 2004, she had suffered several miscarriages and Aniston, to be sure, lent comfort. Once her pal had successfully conceived, Aniston was captivated by what was to come. A witness at an Oscar party in 2004 reported that as the mother-to-be discussed her pregnancy, "[Jennifer] was hanging on everything she said. It was as if she was experiencing it for herself through her words."

Cox is eager for Aniston to have her own taste of motherhood, and is confident her friend will be successful at it. "Jennifer is going to make an amazing mom," she told *Allure*. "She has a huge, huge heart. You never have to wonder where you stand with her. She's completely loyal. Even if she disagrees with you, she stands behind you. I think all those things will make her a great mom. They sure make her a great friend. I love, love, love her."

But long before Monica, there was a friend named Andrea. While Aniston was a drama student at Fiorello H. LaGuardia High School of Music & Art and Performing Arts in New York City (the school in *Fame*), she forged a special bond with classmate Andrea Bendewald. "We took acting very seriously," Bendewald (who later guest-starred on a 2001 episode of *Friends*) said in British *Elle* in 2000. "Acting, studying and boys." What they didn't have in common were looks: "We were such a cliché," Aniston recalled to *Allure* in 2004. "She was tall and skinny and smart. And I was her funny little buddy." Countered Bendewald, "Don't let her fool you. The boys always thought she was beautiful back then."

Of course, it was more than beauty that drew people to the future celebrity. Her chattiness, not to mention her troubled childhood, she explained to the British magazine, landed her "the role of therapist among my friends. Who knows if that comes from being in a family where the parents were more like children that you were? You kind of want to take care of everyone, which can be a bad thing, trying to be a savior for everyone. You kind of miss out on letting them take care of you."

Once she moved to L.A., her warm personality impressed a new group, including Kristin Hahn, her neighbor in a low-rent Laurel Canyon development, where she first lived. "She had that sweet glow about her," Hahn, a documentary film maker and writer, remembered in 2000. "She just oozed love and she still does." When Oprah Winfrey asked Aniston, who has said she especially enjoys buying gifts for people, what she considered her own best qualities as a friend, she responded, "Loyalty. Trust. Honesty. And I guess I'm nurturing, maybe overly so. I also throw a good party." According to Kudrow, she "is just one big throbbing heart."

Although Hahn admits being jealous of Aniston's new life when she hit it big on *Friends*, the star didn't allow fame to interfere with — or ruin — her friendships. "I think the wonderful thing about Jen is that she didn't become well known and then suddenly adopt another lot of friends who are fabulous," said Hahn. "She's kept the things she's had since she was 19." Adulthood, however, hasn't stopped the longtime friends from acting like teenagers. "We do all sorts of crazy things," Aniston admitted to Winfrey. "We howl at the moon — we're those kind of nutter butters." Added the actress, "I've always wanted good friendships and I was inspired to create them by watching my mom with her girlfriends."

No doubt Pitt's long-lasting relationships also had an impact on his wife. One of his dearest friends is actress Catherine Keener, his costar in the 1991 film *Johnny Suede*. "She is incredible. We love her," he told a partygoer after the actress organized the John Kerry screening in L.A. Double-dates with the actress and her husband, actor Dermot Mulroney, were a frequent occurrence for the Pitts. On a few occasions, Pitt and Keener even hit the town by themselves: In 2002, she accompanied the actor to an L.A. Lakers playoffs game. "I was there as a guest of his wife; she gave me her ticket," Keener later said. "I felt like I won the lottery." In 2004, the pair walked the red carpet at the Hollywood premiere of the indie film *Criminal*, produced by Pitt's pals George Clooney and Steven Soderbergh.

So just how good-natured a friend is Pitt? Mulroney was an associate producer of the 1995 comedy *Living in Oblivion*, which poked fun at low-budget indie films. Word was the inspiration for the movie (which also starred Keener) was little-seen *Johnny Suede*. But Mulroney has admitted he wasn't concerned Pitt would be offended. "In my opinion, we made fun of everybody," he has said. "And believe me, Brad is in on the joke."

In 1996, Pitt became the center of another friend's controversy. This time, it was singer/songwriter Melissa Etheridge, whom he met when he first arrived in L.A. (he slept on

her couch). Etheridge, a lesbian, made headlines when she announced that her then-part-
ner Julie Cypher, a video and film director, was
pregnant. (Daughter Bailey was born later that
year.) At the time, the couple would not discuss how Cypher conceived and declined to
reveal the identity of the father. But that didn't
stop the public from speculating that Pitt was
the sperm donor — something the women
found amusing. "We called him up and said,
'Congratulations, Brad, you're a daddy!' "
Etheridge joked. "All you can do is just laugh
about it. But it is absolutely not Brad." (The father, as they later revealed was the anti-Pitt:
Balding, overweight legendary rocker David
Crosby, who also fathered the couple's son
Beckett, born in 1998.) Over the years, Aniston grew close to Etheridge as well, and even
made a cameo in her video for the song "I
Want to Be in Love," also starring the singer's
then-girlfriend (now wife), actress Tammy
Lynn Michaels.

Etheridge is also close with Keener and
Mulroney, and the whole gang often social-
ized. "We hang out and play silly games like
dominoes, charades and Ping-Pong," said
Keener. Afterward, she said, the group might
exercise their musical talents: Etheridge pro-

vided the vocals, Mulroney (an accomplished cellist) played his mandolin, and Pitt and Aniston played bongos or guitar.

Of course, not all of Pitt's friends are artsy musicians or indie actors. Since filming *Ocean's Eleven* and *Ocean's Twelve*, he has become close with costar George Clooney. During a break in the filming of the sequel, the guys, costar Matt Damon, and their significant others even vacationed at Clooney's Lake Como villa. "They're just very, very, you know, kind of down-to-earth guys," Damon said of the megastar pals.

Though both Pitt and Clooney are in their forties, when they're together, they often behave like mischievous little boys. Perhaps it's Clooney's fault: He's a notorious practical joker. But it was Pitt's turn to play mastermind during the 2004 shoot in Italy. He drew up a fake memo to the crew, telling them to address Clooney as 'Mr. Ocean,' the name of his character. It took three weeks before a very confused Clooney finally figured out what was going on. (No doubt Pitt can anticipate payback.) Aniston, according to a source, did not approve of her husband's relationship with the fun-loving bachelor. Said a source close to Pitt, "Jen doesn't like George very much and hated Brad hanging out with him."

A more recent addition to Pitt's posse is Rande Gerber, who is married to Cindy Crawford. The two men are said to be working on a new Las Vegas hotel together, although they have become social friends as well. "Brad really bonded with their kids [Presley and Kaya]," said a Gerber pal. That, however, was not good news for Aniston, who focused on work instead of starting a family. "Once or twice, he and Aniston went to see Rande and Cindy at their place in L.A. and [Brad would] say things to Jen like, 'Look, Cindy has a career and kids, so why can't you?'"

To make matters worse, Aniston was apparently aware of tabloid rumors that Gerber cheated on Crawford (a charge he denied). "Jennifer had heard enough of them to want her husband to stay away from him," said a source close to Pitt.

CHAPTER 8

Two Good to be True

At the start of 2002, the golden couple had learned the golden rule: A couple that plays together — especially in Hollywood — stays together.

Starting at The Sundance Film Festival on January 12, the twosome caused a frenzy when they arrived in the mountain town of Park City, Utah. Aniston was there to promote *The Good Girl*, "the feel weird movie of the year," as she put it. Hundreds of fans stood outside the Eccles Theatre trying to catch a glimpse of her and Pitt, as well as the festival's founder (and Pitt's *Spy Game* costar) Robert Redford.

Pitt, meanwhile, had just begun what would be a hiatus from making movies (though, at the time, he had started growing a beard for Darren Aronofsky's sci-fi epic *The Fountain*). Eight days later, he and Aniston were back to their Hollywood roots, attending the 59th annual Golden Globe Awards at the Beverly Hills Hilton. They turned up in stylishly matching black pant suits (hers was Dolce & Gabbana), sat next to Courteney Cox and David Arquette, and remained gracious losers as *Friends* failed to take home the trophy for any of its nominated categories.

Once again, Pitt pulled out the romantic stops on Aniston's February 11 birthday. For number thirty-three, he surprised her with a $10,000 party at the hot Hollywood sushi spot Katana on Sunset Boulevard. When it was dessert time, he presented her with a miniature replica of the couple's six-tiered wedding cake. After giving her a platinum charm bracelet from Harry Winston (reportedly worth $5,000), he raised his glass for the gathering. "You're my best friend," he toasted. "My soul mate, the one I'll spend eternity with."

As Pitt doted on his wife, Aniston enjoyed a career peak. In its eighth season, *Friends* garnered its highest ratings in years (some TV experts credited the resurgence to post-9/11 entertainment "comfort food"). Though the cast's $750,000-an-episode contracts were all set to expire, the sexy sextet quickly negotiated to shoot a ninth and, at the time, final season. Their paycheck: A whopping $1 million an episode for twenty-four shows. (Jerry Seinfeld and Paul Reiser and Helen Hunt were the only other sitcom stars to ever pull in that kind of money, for *Seinfeld* and *Mad About You*, respectively). The *Friends* juggernaut rolled along until the May season finale, when Rachel gave birth to a daughter, named Emma. Onlookers reported that Aniston cried during the labor scene, only fueling off-camera pregnancy rumors.

Otherwise, the couple got in their share of summer lovin'. They continued spending quiet nights indoors playing board games and watching reality TV with their friends. In June, Aniston and Cox threw a fortieth birthday party for their manager, Cynthia Pett-Dante, at Cox's Malibu home. It was a girls-only affair for forty guests, including Renée Zellweger and Elizabeth Perkins — until Pitt crashed it.

By late July, with the couple seemingly inseparable, came a double-dose of good news: It was announced that Aniston earned an Emmy nomination for the first time in the Outstanding Lead Actress in a Comedy Series category, and Pitt got a nod for Outstanding Guest Actor in a Comedy Series for his 2001 *Friends* cameo appearance. "Brad and I were sleeping when we heard the news," the actress said. "I was very excited and giddy. It took him a day to figure it out. He was a little shocked by the whole thing. I think he never even expected [his nomination] was a possibility. I think he even forgot. But it was great because we had so much fun doing it and it was the last thing you would ever expect."

Call it a case of perfect timing. Days later, the couple celebrated their two-year anniversary — in private. "We had a lovely day," she simply stated. (It was reported, however, that she gave him a stack of the racy *Girls Gone Wild* DVDs). But the couple didn't completely close off their relationship from the public. "I'll tell you about his laugh," she said in a first person article in *Esquire*. "I don't know how to explain it except it sounds like a 12-year-old boy who just threw a water balloon down on somebody. Just the other night, he was watching the Robin Williams HBO special while I was sending out e-mails in another room, and out burst that great mischievous laugh. I just looked up and giggled."

The Good Girl was released nationwide in early August, and it quickly earned Aniston the best reviews of her big-screen career and prompted Oscar buzz. Suddenly, the industry regarded Aniston as more than the ditzy *Friends* star with the hunky husband. She was a bona fide actress who could effortlessly transform herself into a Texas woman with a dead-end job and a dead-end husband. Several outlets dubbed Aniston "The Mary Tyler Moore" of this generation. "It felt like an opportunity to go out on a limb — a terrifying opportunity — to go out on a limb," she told *Time* of her *Good Girl* role.

Pitt's main project? Growing out his beard for *The Fountain*, which was scheduled to go into production in Australia that fall with Cate Blanchett as a costar. Contrary to reports, Aniston was a fan of the Abraham Lincoln-like facial hair. "It's gotten past the prickly part," she said in *USA Today*. "It's very soft and he conditions it. Sometimes I'll just start twirling it as we're watching a movie." Nonetheless, the film was scrapped in early fall. "I helped him shave it," said Aniston in a magazine of the beard, which quickly went the way of *The Fountain*. "We did all sorts of facial designs as it got less and less. There was the Amish look, the bounty hunter thing, the French guy…"

Indeed, the marriage had hit its stride. The couple practically glowed when they hit the red carpet hand-in-hand for the 54th annual Emmy Awards on September 22. It was Aniston's big night, but Pitt almost missed her shining moment. Decked in a pink beaded Christian Dior dress, Aniston sat nervously in the front row next to Pitt, clutching his hand

and kicking her foot as she anticipated the award for her category.

Then, during a commercial break, the actor suddenly bolted for the men's room. After the quickie pit stop (and an even quicker autograph session for female fans in the lobby), he returned in time to give his wife a congratulatory kiss for snagging her first Emmy. A teary Aniston thanked her beloved *Friends* costars and her husband. A few moments later, the sitcom won for Outstanding Comedy Series for the first time. "It's a delicious cake and now we're eating it — and now there's icing on top," she said afterward. A backstage observer reported, "As happy as she was, there was a sense of calm about her. As if she was holding back." At the post-Emmy party in the downtown L.A. eatery Zucca, party-goers erupted into cheers when Aniston and her cast mates entered with their awards. This time, the newlyweds did not leave each other's side.

The two tried to go on with their lives as normally as possible — but as Hollywood's most photographed couple, it was more wishful thinking than reality. During one October excursion to Studio Hexagon, a furniture store in West Hollywood, they attracted such a crowd of fans that two sheriff's deputies had to escort them to their car. (They fared better shortly thereafter at the opening of Salma Hayek's brother Sami's furniture store in L.A.) In November, Pitt took a pre-Thanksgiving solo trip to Springfield, where paparazzi madness stood at a minimum.

To relax — and, perhaps, keep up appearances — the couple went on regular getaway trips to the Ojai Valley Inn & Spa just outside L.A. for facials, peels, and massages (Aniston even got the peach fuzz waxed off her face). "They always request a $2,500-per-night penthouse suite," said one source. Not that all the trips were R&R for the stars: "Poor Jennifer's cell phone literally rings off the hook. If she turns it off for an hour, she'll have 20 messages to return!"

In fact, the Pitts were busier than ever. In December, it was reported that the two had signed on to bring the best-selling coming-of-age memoir *My Losing Season* by Pat Conroy to the big screen. Pitt planned to co-produce and Aniston was set to co-executive produce the project, although it never came to fruition. Pitt, who made a cameo in Clooney's directorial debut, *Confessions of a Dangerous Mind*, had agreed to star as the Greek hero Achilles in the big-budget war epic *Troy* and started bulking up his body for the role. Aniston, meanwhile, wrapped the Jim Carrey vehicle *Bruce Almighty* and signed on to star in a comedy with Ben Stiller.

What would the future entail for the Golden Couple? It didn't matter, as long as they had each other.

CHAPTER 9

Their Dream Home

The Pitt's adventures in real estate began with a small-scale purchase (well, small, for them). In December 2000, the newlyweds bought a $4 million commune in Santa Barbara. Reported one source, "Jennifer was more than a little skeptical, but Brad was convinced it could be their personal paradise." The cottages were falling apart, and dust and sand were everywhere. "It was in shambles," said the source.

Despite no formal training, the actor had a passion for architecture. Among his heroes: legendary designer Frank Gehry. "He said to me 'If you know where it's going, it's not worth doing.' That's become like a mantra for me," he told *Vanity Fair* "That's the life of the artist. The life of the artist is not about sure success. Gehry didn't have a hit till he was 60." He added, "I may still [become an architect]. I just want to make things." It's a talent that Aniston completely respected. "My sweet, dear husband, who has such patience with me, the idiot savant, is inherently brilliant with homes, structure," she said in *Vogue*. "I had a hard time with it at first because I felt a little bit inferior because for me, it's not about the hippest thing, it's about what feels the best."

With an eye for the aesthetically pleasing, Pitt spent more time planning the renovation than he did making movies. Soon, under his supervision, the oceanfront estate was slowly but surely converted into a weekend haven. Palm trees and grass were planted. A five-foot-deep above-ground swimming pool was installed.

The compound transformation wasn't 100% completed until September 2004. But the new renovations were magnificent. In Guest House #1, visitors — which have included Courteney Cox and David Arquette, Edward Norton, and Melissa Etheridge — enjoyed two bedrooms, a gym with a StairMaster, treadmill, and free weights, as well as a kitchenette. Guest House # 2 featured a flat-screen TV, DVD library, a stack of board games (like Twister), and beanbag chairs. The master suite included a "Moroccan Room" decorated with yellow walls and a single mattress on the floor. A source said it was Pitt's favorite space.

But the couple's retreat was just a warm-up act for what was to come. "Brad's a land man,"

Aniston said in *W*. "He wants land, land, land." For months, the couple searched for a spacious mansion with, yes, lots of land, and a view of the Pacific Ocean. "They were looking for a home to settle in and have their kids," said a source. "They planned to live there for the long haul." In June 2001, one month before Aniston and Pitt celebrated their first anniversary, they purchased their dream home in Beverly Hills. Although Aniston once remarked, "I'm not going to tell how much it cost," experts put the price at $12 to 14 million. They closed escrow one month later.

Ironically, the 12,000-square-foot mansion — which sat on slightly more than an acre of land at the end of a cul-de-sac — had no ocean view. But the attributes were hardly in short supply. "It's beautiful, with sloping grounds, a tennis court and a lot of privacy," said a source. Built in 1934 for actor Fredric March, the recently restored French Normandy-style home had six bedrooms, including a master suite with his and hers sitting rooms, six-and-a-half baths, and a rotunda foyer. Sources also added that when the couple toured the home (with Courteney Cox along for the ride), Aniston was particularly attracted to the fact that one of the dressing rooms would make a perfect nursery. A witness reported that Pitt said affectionately, "You got it, Jen bear."

The late architect Wallace Neff designed the home, and his son, Wallace Jr., remarked, "The house reeks of beauty, charm and elegance." Amongst the amenities were a massive fireplace (a trademark of Neff's); a "taproom" that doubles as a screening room; and a wine cellar with an adjoining dining area (in additional to the formal dining room). The Pitt's master suite featured his-and-her offices and dressing rooms, a fireplace, and a terrace that overlooked the grounds, as well as the sweeping views of the Hollywood Hills. Once outside, the couple could take advantage of a waterfall pool, cabana and a tennis court with rest rooms.

But for the Pitts, the dream home was only a dream in theory. They quickly decided to make some internal changes, and bunked in Aniston's cozy Hollywood Hills pad in the interim. "At first, we said, 'We'll just redo the floor and the master bedroom,'" Aniston explained in O. "We ended up breaking down walls. It was symbolic of building our relationship."

Indeed, initially Aniston didn't mind the changes. "He definitely has strong opinions about aesthetics, and I admire that," she said in *W*. "It's hard, though, because the one thing I thought I could do well was put homes together, but it's something that really matters to him, so we've learned to make decisions that we both feel good about. And I actually think our marriage is even better now because we've been through this stuff. We've settled in; we've survived the whole house-construction aspect, and that's a big thing. It's not always easy. It takes work."

March 2002 was their target move-in date. It didn't happen. Instead of a few minor changes, they decided to do a complete renovation. "It's currently unlivable," an insider said. Meanwhile, their Santa Barbara weekend retreat was also still being worked on. "I think Jennifer considers weekends there sort of glorified camping," said a worker on the house. "It is still virtually three shacks."

As she promoted *The Good Girl* in the summer of 2002, the strain had begun to show. "God, no," she replied, when asked if she had moved in yet. "We kind of…we gutted it. Once you start, my lovely architectural husband gets in there…" Pitt, for his part, was unforgiving about the changes. "I just couldn't keep my hands off it," he said in *Vanity Fair*.

"I'm gonna build from the ground up — I have to."

Among Pitt's changes: A stone fireplace in the home movie theater; an open, oval stone shower; rare onyx tiles in Aniston's private bathroom — plus a separate shampoo room with a salon-style sink. (Aniston later denied the shampoo room's existence). Most notably a nursery with green walls and a kitchen with heated floors ("so Jen can stay warm during a pregnancy," said a source) were in the works. "We call it The Room," Aniston explained of the nursery in *Allure*. "Brad's waited a long time for kids."

In spring 2003, the estimated $1 million home improvement project reached its not-so-happy two-year anniversary. "The design of the house was Brad's job, but the rest was a team effort, which is why it took so long," the actress explained in the same interview. "We had to agree on every thing." The couple checked the progress of the mansion on a weekly basis. On April 24, they even brought along soon-to-be neighbors Danny DeVito and wife Rhea Perlman, who lived in the same cul-de-sac, to inspect the property. "[Brad] was unhappy with the floors," said a source familiar with the renovations. "He didn't like the color of the wood, so he had it ripped out and redone." De-Vito was more sympathetic: "They're my good friends," he said. "I did the same thing with my house. It takes awhile and can be costly, but you do what you have to do."

Despite the demands of detail-oriented Pitt and the setbacks, including complaints from neighbors that construction vehicles were clogging surrounding streets (the Pitts wound up shuttling workers to and from the property each day in buses), workers estimated that the renovations would be finished within months. "If I was God for a week, I'd have the house finished," said Aniston, referring to Jim Carrey's fictional powers in her smash hit movie, *Bruce Almighty*. "I do believe it when they say that if you can survive building a house to-gether you can survive anything."

But for Aniston, the end of the construc-tion tunnel meant she'd have to bid adieu to her beloved two-bedroom Hollywood Hills bungalow that she'd owned for eight years. "I'm [going to have to] sell my house," she said. "It kind of breaks my heart, but it's a whole new chapter." In the end, she wound up holding on to it. At the time of the split, it was being rented by British comic Sacha Baron Cohen, a.k.a. Ali G.

Finally, on July 2, moving vans arrived at the couple's old home and carted off furniture to their newly remodeled digs. With Pitt knee-deep in the production of *Troy* in Mexico, it was up to Aniston to feather the nest. By combining her homey, comfortable instincts with his knack for the sleek, austere, and stylish she pulled the job off, filling the house with French Modern furniture by Jean-Michel Frank and Pierre Chareau. "Brad has opened me up to a whole new world of auctions and antiques," she said. "When I see a strictly modern home, I find it very cold and uninviting. [When decorating] I go first with what feels good, and that isn't always right."

Still, Aniston had one primary reservation of Pitt's preference for marble, stone, and hard edges — including a glass table. "It's not very kid-friendly," she said in *Allure*. "But we've had babies of friends over to test it, and the tough ones survive banging their heads on the stone floors."

"You gotta fall down," Pitt later responded in *Vanity Fair*. "You gotta learn."

For two modest celebrities, the scope of the mansion also took some time to get used to. "When Brad and I walk into our house, we still giggle," Aniston said months after moving day in *O*. "I loved having a small house…That makes me happy." Seconded Pitt in *Vanity Fair*, "We're still like a couple of kids squatting in some Beverly Hills mansion." And, as Aniston wryly noted on *Primetime Live*, "We love being in the same room. It's funny. We got a house with more rooms, and yet we still stay in the same room together."

By 2004, as the couple settled into their retreat, they concluded that their two-year headache had only strengthened their bond. "My home has always been my prized possession, it was always the thing that I did great," Aniston said in *Vogue* in 2004. "There was a lot of 'Honey, what do you think?' And now we have a house that is truly a combination of both of us, and it's beautiful. At the end of it, it was the greatest thing we ever did… Next to making a kid, and then the house will be the second-best thing we ever did."

CHAPTER 10

The Trouble Begins

For more than two years, Jennifer Aniston and Brad Pitt — successful, gorgeous, rich, and hopelessly in love — reigned as Hollywood's definitive, larger-than-life couple. But as their popularity grew, so did their stress of being under the public's microscope.

By January 2003, every time the Pitts went out in public — which was a semi-rare event in itself — they faced the scrutiny. There was the inevitable when-are-you-having-a-baby question; *The Good Girl* Oscar buzz (would Aniston get nominated?); and the hoopla surrounding the late December announcement that Aniston and her pals would film a tenth and final season of *Friends* for $1 million an episode. The barrage was enough to drive them crazy.

Or, at least, drive them out of the country. The couple — along with Courteney Cox and David Arquette (and Pitt's assistant and her fiancé) — took a five-day trip to Mexico in early January. It wasn't a complete disaster, but it was hardly a second honeymoon, either. The women often went off by themselves, as they enjoyed workouts at a nearby gym and a house call from a personal masseuse. The men, meanwhile, chartered a fishing boat and went snorkeling.

Aniston and Pitt, meanwhile, kept the displays of affection private, never held hands or looked too cozy. According to one cab driver, as the group traveled from the San Jose de Cabo airport to their villa outside the city (at the exclusive gated community of Villas de Mar), Pitt and Aniston did not kiss, hug, or even hold hands in the back seat. And a saleswoman at the Villas del Mar reported that she never saw the couple get romantic.

Upon returning to Los Angeles, the couple added even more fuel to the proverbial trouble-in-paradise fire. In January, Aniston turned up stag at The People's Choice Awards in the Pasadena Civic Auditorium, where she won a trophy for Favorite Female Television Performer. Though the event was hardly a must-attend, Aniston curiously sat beside a random seat-filler, which led some to assume producers held out hope that Pitt would make a last-minute appearance.

The same week, she was quoted in the new issue of *W* magazine questioning whether Pitt was her soul mate. "Is he the love of my life?"

she hesitantly mused. "I think you're always sort of wondering, 'Are you the love of my life?' I mean, I don't know. I've never been someone who says, 'He's the love of my life' He's certainly a big love in my life." (The comment drew so much outcry, Diane Sawyer grilled Aniston about it one year later during a *Primetime Live* interview. Her reply: "I didn't hesitate. That was something I hated reading. I can't imagine being with any other human being. I married him because he was the love of my life. So when these things are written in magazines and taken out of context, it's so frustrating 'cause people then take it and run with it.")

The curious behavior reached its peak at the Golden Globe Awards on January 19. To the disappointment of fans, photographers, and the media, the couple turned up on the red carpet mysteriously late — and, with literally minutes to spare, had time to do just one rushed TV interview (that lasted under thirty seconds). Backstage, Aniston blamed the tardiness on "a dress dilemma. I was stressed and we had to drive all the way around the block."

Almost immediately after they settled into their seats at the *Friends* table, Aniston had to take the stage to accept a trophy for Best Actress in a Comedy Series. Pulling her flustered self together with the aid of a cane (she broke a toe on her right foot), she gave an appreciative speech: "Thank you. Thank you, Foreign Press. Thank you. I have to thank these five people: Matthew Perry, David Schwimmer, Lisa Kudrow, Courteney Cox and Matt LeBlanc. I love you guys. You started out as my colleagues, and you're my friends — and you're my family."

One small problem: She did not thank her husband of more than two years, who beamed with pride nearby. Even worse, cameras caught the disappointed look on Pitt's face after Aniston finished her speech. Of course, Aniston wasn't the first actress to forget to thank a spouse during an acceptance speech — Hilary Swank blanked on Chad Lowe when she won a Best Actress Oscar in 2000 and Sarah Jessica Parker snubbed Matthew Broderick at the Golden Globes in 2002 — but she was certainly the most high-profile. Was it a simple slip or a telltale sign of marital strife?

Aniston realized the gaffe and immediately went into spin control for an hour backstage. "I forgot to thank my husband, like a nincompoop!" Aniston told Matt Lauer. "And I love you, Brad Pitt, and I thank you so much." To

Entertainment Tonight: "Can I just say that I love Brad Pitt? I love you!" After the awards, the couple stopped by a small party at the Beverly Hills Hilton, but they left within minutes — reportedly because Aniston, though a newly minted winner, wanted to go home.

Though only Aniston knew what was really going on, perhaps there was an external reason for her gloom: That pesky broken toe, which she busted after hitting it on a piece of furniture. "Having a broken bone in a foot is extremely painful and may have affected her mood," said New York City podiatrist Dr. Rock Positano. "The average person takes 10,000 to 15,000 steps a day. You try putting your foot down with that much pain all the time and you wouldn't be in a very good mood, either."

A more likely explanation for the couple's unhappiness was the lack of the pitter-patter of little Pitts. Sources said that Brad, on the verge of his fortieth birthday, had become increasingly anxious to have children. "We want to start a family," he said in January 2003. "But it's not like we have a date set for that."

Aniston, meanwhile, had always maintained that procreation would start after *Friends* wrapped, so it was a mild surprise when the cast suddenly renegotiated their contracts. But the *New York Post* reported that Aniston, in an effort to appease her impatient husband, insisted on a shortened eighteen-episode season that would wrap months ahead of schedule. Her rep said this was false, but a *Friends* source confirmed that she did "express interest" in the shortened season. "She will start a family after *Friends*. She will also produce with Brad and star in some films," said the source. Added another, "I'm sure it's true she wants to start a family, so that's why she wasn't crazy about doing a full season of the show."

Other friends of the couple defended their struggles and claimed they had simply experienced the usual growing pains. "People are making too much about them not having babies," said the *Friends* source. "How many other couples who have been married two years have started families? … It's unfair to put any married couple through the kind of pressure they go through." Another *Friends* source insisted, "She's extremely happy these days. I don't think they have any more trouble finding time to be together than most working couples do."

Aniston, for her part, dismissed any dust-ups. In the same interview in which she questioned Pitt as the love of her life, she also remarked about the relatively peaceful state of their union. "We do fight," she said in *W*. "Well, we have discussions. I am not a fan of fighting when it is screaming. I like accomplishing something. But I don't trust a couple that says they don't fight." She waxed even more about her husband's kindness: "He'll hate me for saying that ... but when you grow up in a family where people are not always very kind to each other, you realize how important that is."

The Golden Couple

*Brad and Jen celebrate at a post Academy Awards celebration in
2000, the same year they were married. Their eventual breakup would
rival all other headlines at the beginning of 2005.*

Brad and Gwyneth Paltrow attend a movie premiere in 1997 shortly before their relationship ended.

Brad, after a legendary drive to Hollywood with $325 in his pocket and stardom in his sight, finally found his breakout role as the cowboy stud in Thelma and Louise in 1991.

Jen poses with boyfriend Tate Donovan in 1997, who went on to appear on the hit series The O.C.

The cast of Friends from the show's first season: (clockwise from left) Matt Le Blanc as Joey, Lisa Kudrow as Phoebe, David Schwimmer as Ross, Matthew Perry as Chandler, Jennifer Aniston as Rachel, and Courtney Cox as Monica.

In 1998, the hottest thing coming out of the Tibetan Festival in Washington D.C. were photographs of Pitt and Aniston nuzzling back-stage. The shots made news across the globe as fans celebrated the union of two of Hollywood's most popular celebrities.

The couple showed off Jen's engagement ring onstage during a Sting concert in November of 1999.

Michael Sanville/WireImage.com

Photo by Damiani/ZUMA Press

A Day to Remember

Brad and Jen, perfect on the big screen or in black-and-white snapshots, enjoy a moment after their wedding in Malibu, California, on July 29, 2000. Pitt personally helped to design their wedding rings in white gold with diamonds.

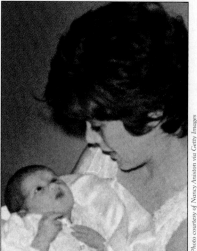

Photo courtesy of Nancy Aniston via Getty Images

Nancy Aniston holds her new daughter shortly after Jennifer's birth in 1969.

Courtesy of South Haven Baptist Church

The Pitt family of Springfield, Missouri (from left to right — Doug, Bill, Brad, Jane, and Julie) in 1985, years before Brad became a member of Hollywood's A-list leading men.

Courtney Cox poses with the Golden Couple at a 2003 benefit for A.L.S. disease. Courtney and her husband David Arquette became the Pitt's most trusted friends.

Friends co-star Matt LeBlanc intimately says goodbye after a lunch in Los Angeles in 2004.

Nina Prommer/Globe Photos, Inc.

Red Carpet Sensation
Brad and Jen show off their star power at the Emmy Awards in Los Angeles in 2000.

Stefano Rellandini/Reuters

The couple made a fashion statement of their own at the Armani men's collection in Milan in 2001.

Brad's guest appearance on the 2001 Thanksgiving episode of Friends won him an Emmy nomination.

The couple (despite admitting to be most comfortable in more casual attire) makes a grand appearance on the red carpet at the 2002 Emmy Awards. Jen would win her one and only Emmy for playing Rachel on Friends that evening.

Pitt, in a typical show of affection, cozies up to his wife at the Golden Globes in 2002.

Jen, after winning a Golden Globe in 2003, forgot to thank Brad in her emotional acceptance speech, fueling rumors the marriage was on the rocks.

The couple bought and redesigned a multi-million dollar home in Bel Air, California…

… and another compound in Santa Barbara, California.

In 2004 Brad spent months away from Jen while filming the $180,000,000 epic Troy.

Branching out for the movie The Good Girl in 2002, Jen received positive reviews for her portrayal of Justine, a poor young woman who has to deal with an unexpected pregnancy.

Paul Smith/Featureflash/Retna Ltd.

The couple attends the gala screening of his movie Troy at the Cannes Film Festival in May, 2004.

Jeff Kravitz/FilmMagic.com

In what may be their last public appearance as husband and wife, Brad and Jen sat side by side in 2004 at the Emmy Awards.

More than Friends?

While filming Mr. and Mrs. Smith in Rome during October 2004, Brad and Angelina Jolie reportedly spent lots of time together — both on camera and off. Jolie has countered that she didn't need the headache of dating a married man.

Jen and co-star Clive Owen make it through a downpour in a scene from Derailed, filmed while Brad was on location in Rome.

A Kiss Goodbye
Brad and Jen take a stroll on a Caribbean beach on January 6, 2005.
The next day, they announced that they were ending their marriage.

A Love Affair to Remember
Brad and Jen at the Independent Spirit Awards in 2003

CHAPTER 11

Celebrity Coupling: Can it Ever Work?

"Here's one thing I know about love: The greater your capacity to love, the greater the capacity to feel pain," Aniston told O Magazine, almost a year before her breakup. "I know for sure that it hurts — and yet I love it."

But when two starry-eyed stars fall for each other, the relationship can be even more painful. Aside from the glare of the unrelenting media spotlight, couples must deal with long separations, frenetic schedules, nasty gossip, and the constant nagging to have genetically blessed children. Even more challenging, they have to delicately balance two superstar egos. In retrospect, did two megapopular celebrities like Aniston and Pitt ever have a chance at staying happily married?

"Hollywood couples — like Brad and Jen — are expected to be perfect all they time," says Dr. Carole Lieberman, author of *Bad Boys: Why We Love Them, How to Live with Them, When to Leave Them*. "There is always that pressure, which leads couples to hide their problems. [Sometimes] it can lead to the feeling that if things *weren't* perfect, something must be really wrong with the marriage." Factor in a celebrity's insecurities and pressures, and the problems only manifest themselves. Says Dr. Elizabeth Saenger, "A lot of the time, the public feeds someone's narcissism and a person can believe the world revolves around them. While that may be nice for a career, it may just be a pain in the butt for your partner. It leads to big trouble. There is always the risk of not having enough communication to keep a marriage solid."

But according to Dr. Drew Pinsky, psychiatrist and host of the radio show *Strictly Sex with Dr. Drew*, fame is only one small factor in a couple's public demise. "Whatever pathologies people have in their lives all come to the surface when they're famous," he says. "Fame doesn't cause [problems]. It's an issue of whether people can work through stressors and pay attention to the needs of a relationship."

So who among Aniston and Pitt's A-list peers defied the mounting odds and continues to thrive in a happy relationship — and who didn't? When reviewing Hollywood relationships, role models are hard to find. Victims are plenty.

Reese Witherspoon and Ryan Phillippe

From the time Witherspoon, twenty-eight, and Phillippe, thirty, met at her twenty-first birthday party in Los Angeles in March 1997 (he has said he went for the free drinks), it seemed unlikely that the two rising stars would ultimately become poster children for Hollywood family values. But the Tennessee Southern belle was pregnant when the two wed in 1999 and daughter Ava was born three months later.

Then, in spite of Witherspoon's hot career — just months after giving birth, she was nominated for a Golden Globe for her breakout starring role in the critically acclaimed comedy *Election*— they devised a plan allowing them both to work without sacrificing their new family. "We go back and forth with which one of us wants to take another job," she explained. On October 23, 2003, Witherspoon gave birth to a son, Deacon. Hands-on parents, they take turns making their children breakfast and taking them to the park. "For me, having [children] is like having a second childhood," she said. And Phillippe has been quoted as saying, "I did have my time when I was no angel. But now I just want to keep my family happy."

Nonetheless, the pair has worked tirelessly to keep their marriage strong. In 2002, Phillippe admitted that they attended couples counseling. "We're normal people with normal problems," said Witherspoon. They also had to uproot from their English Tudor-style mansion in the Hollywood Hills to Wales for months while Witherspoon, who commands $15 million a movie, filmed 2003's period drama *Vanity Fair* and Phillippe acted in the World War II tale *Light in the Sky*. And they still make time to celebrate their anniversaries — like the one they spent on June 5, 2003, when they enjoyed a romantic dinner at London's Nobu. "They are very much still in love," says a source. "It's obvious from the way they look at each other."

Gwen Stefani and Gavin Rossdale

The California-reared No Doubt singer and the British Bush front man met in 1995 when her band opened for his band. ("He liked me first!" she said). Their six-year courtship was a bumpy one: In 1999, amid rumors of his infidelities, they split for a week. (Stefani dyed her hair pink). One year later, he was briefly linked to Irish singer Andrea Corr, and they split again. "I wish I had a little leash to walk

Gavin around," she said. And their times spent together were at a premium. "The only reason we've been successful is we've been able to afford it, first of all," she has said of the transatlantic plane trips.

But on New Year's Day 2002, Rossdale popped the question with a diamond ring he purchased in Amsterdam. "I based my life on not being traditional," he said. "I guess getting married is my most traditional move yet! But that's cool. I haven't looked back." The two wed on September 14 in London's St. Paul church in front of 130 guests, then celebrated with a reception in Beverly Hills two weeks later.

The two enjoyed a few smooth years, and in 2004, Rossdale stayed by his wife's side while she promoted her debut solo CD, Love, Angel, Music, Baby. On the rare off days they hung out with friends like Aniston and Pitt, and took walks in the park with their beloved Puli dog, Winston.

In October 2004 came a setback: A DNA test proved Rossdale was the father of a fifteen-year-old girl, Daisy Lowe (also his godchild), whose mother, Pearl, was a friend. "Gavin insisted that he had never slept with Pearl," said a source.

Even faced with these challenges, they are still together. Pals said Stefani has pressed Rossdale to attend counseling. After all, she has never hid her desire to be a mom. "I'll make one more album, then I'll get pregnant," she announced in 2002. For now, Stefani is standing by her man.

As she wrote in the 2001 No Doubt song, "Underneath It All": "You've used up all your coupons… And somehow I'm full of forgiveness."

Kate Hudson and Chris Robinson

When Hudson and Robinson wed at her mother Goldie Hawn's Aspen, Colorado, home in December 2000, few thought the relationship would last. They had a twelve-year age gap to contend with and there were the contrasting personalities: she's the giggly and glam Oscar-nominated actress; he's the soft-spoken and scruffy lead singer for the Black Crowes. Said Hudson of their first date, "I thought, 'My God, I'm already in love with a man I don't think anybody is going to understand!'"

But the two had lived through broken relationships. He divorced Lala Sloatman in the nineties; she's estranged from her dad, Bill Hudson. They were determined to make it work. In 2003, the actress took a year off from movies to tour with Robinson on his bus and was often spotted beaming from backstage. On Valentine's Day 2003, when he hit Chicago without her, she sent him 200 *I LOVE YOU* balloons. "We will make romance out of any situation," he said.

Their happiness led to a bundle of joy: On January 7, 2004, the two welcomed son Ryder Russell Robinson (who weighed in at 8 pounds, 11 ounces). "They love being parents," said a source. "They're really hands-on and adore the baby." The couple's new neighbors in New York City's West Village reported that they're often spotted cooing over their baby. Said one, "They're always pushing a stroller." Not that the couple seems to mind: "Our whole world is poop!" Hudson said in May 2004. And there might be more on the way — Hudson added she wants "a million babies."

Until then the actress and Robinson are making the most of their off days together despite his recent tour and her newest movies. As Hudson has said, "You have to find time to play together, because life's hard, even if you make a trillion dollars!"

Jessica Simpson and Nick Lachey

Nick Lachey and Jessica Simpson met at a

1999 *Teen People* party, quickly fell in love, and by the time they wed in a lavish Texas ceremony on October 26, 2002, even they would admit that their claim to fame was their status as fading nineties pop singers. A few months later, they agreed to let MTV chronicle their lives for a reality show called *Newlyweds: Nick & Jessica*.

The show — which drew around four million viewers a week — became an overnight success. Fans relished Simpson's ditziness (as in the now-classic "Is this chicken or fish?" moment), Lachey's seemingly eternal patience, and their devotion to each other. "We're going to be married 50 years," he said.

No doubt the show has been good to the twosome, but it was particularly kind to Simpson. She waded through endorsement deals, developed a cosmetics line, filmed an ABC pilot, and nabbed the role as Daisy Duke in the *The Dukes of Hazzard*. Lachey, however, was regarded as a second banana (his first solo CD, SoulO, flopped). But Lachey insisted he harbored no jealousy, "I'm her biggest fan. I want nothing more than to see her succeed."

Indeed, Simpson's first priority remained her husband. She took cooking classes for him, filled their Calabas, California, home with candles and flowers, and gave a sexy performance with the Pussycat Dolls for his thirtieth birthday, to name just a few things. "Romance for me is just being with Nick," she said. "It doesn't have to be an elaborate scenario. We love bubble baths, drinking wine and listing to jazz." A baby wasn't on the agenda — but Lachey presented his wife with a puppy named Daisy on her twenty-fourth birthday.

The end of 2004, however, brought plenty of roadblocks — from Lachey's proximity to a porn star at a pal's bachelor party to Simpson's alleged flirtation with an Abercrombie & Fitch employee in Baton Rouge on the set of *The Dukes of Hazzard* — and things escalated to the point where even their closest friends wondered if the couple was on the verge of splitting. They didn't believe it for a moment. "Our marriage is very, very strong," said Lachey. "I think what's healthy about us is that we don't see eye to eye. We meet halfway. If you're open with each other, it always works." Seconded Simpson, "We want the truth to get out there: There are no problems. We're blissfully in love."

Jennifer Lopez and Ben Affleck

It began so innocently: Affleck and Lopez

met in December 2001 on the set of *Gigli*. He was six months out of rehab for alcohol abuse; she was wed to backup dancer Cris Judd. They got along well — very well. By July 2002, the two were so close, he attended a surprise birthday lunch for her in NYC and gave her a Harry Winston diamond bracelet as a present. One day later, she filed for divorce from Judd. And with that, "Bennifer" was born.

It was the hottest celebrity hookup this side of Britney Spears and Justin Timberlake. Surprisingly, the two were hardly gun-shy about going public with their romance: On August 1, they were photographed in Affleck's new Bentley reading about themselves in *Us Weekly*. Then he appeared as Lopez's boyfriend in her "Jenny from the Block" video (*literally* kissing her derriere). The whirlwind affair peaked in September, when he gave J.Lo a $3.5 million pink diamond ring. Unlike Aniston, Lopez couldn't wait to tell the world about the engagement — she recounted the proposal in detail to Diane Sawyer, where she said, "I was like 'Oh yeah. Yeah, yes, yes!'"

It turned out they didn't always agree. Much to Lopez's dismay, Affleck visited a Vancouver strip club in July and reportedly got cozy with an exotic dancer. ("She was upset," said a source). She also disapproved of his penchant for late-night casino trips and reportedly did not get along with best pal Matt Damon. That *Gigli* opened on August 1 to scathing reviews didn't help matters.

The worse was yet to come: On September 10, just two days before their planned nuptials in Montecito, Calfornia, the couple issued a statement that they were postponing the event because of "the media circus." The real reason may have been an apprehension to give up his bachelorhood. Said a source, "He would roll his eyes anytime his friends brought up the wedding. He wasn't acting like a guy in love." The two claimed that they were not splitting up — the night of the announcement, they dined together at The Ivy under the paparazzi surveillance — but a source explained that Lopez was "heartbroken and devastated" by the decision.

The couple split for good in late January 2004, and, as a result, put an end to the Bennifer frenzy. A close Lopez source said that she had grown increasingly upset by photos of Affleck and Damon taken in Germany surrounded by young women and his inability to set a wedding date ("I'm not going to sit around waiting for anyone," she was overheard defiantly saying one night after the split). Affleck was bothered with her recent Miami rendezvous with exes Sean "P. Diddy" Combs and Marc Anthony. "If you can't change someone, you have to move on," added a source.

And they did: Less than six months after the split, Lopez quietly wed her former flame Marc Anthony in a small, backyard ceremony. Affleck, meanwhile, according to a source, hooked up with his *Daredevil* costar, Jennifer Garner, over the summer of 2004 and, in what's become a rite of passage for all his girlfriends, took her to a Boston Red Sox game in October. But perhaps they are a little wiser in the wake of Bennifer: Neither party talked about their new sweetheart.

Ethan Hawke and Uma Thurman

The relationship began in the most ordinary of places: A New York City ATM. In 1992, Hawke, then a lesser-known actor, tried to talk to the six-foot-beauty without luck. Four years later, they reunited on the set of *Gattaca*. On May 1, 1998, they wed in New York City's St. John the Divine Cathedral. She gave birth to Maya two months later and son Roan was born in 2002.

The red-hot Gen-X duo were always frank about their monogamy. "I'm not worried about him straying. If something happened in our relationship, I'm sure it would be my fault," Thurman once said. And Hawke griped in a 2000 article, "It's f—- hard to get along with somebody... It's work."

Hawke's philosophy was sadly prophetic. In the summer of 2003, it was rumored that he had carried on an alleged affair with a twenty-two-year-old aspiring model and apparel designer named Jennifer Perzow on the Montreal set of *Taking Lives* (Thurman was in Vancouver filming *Paycheck* with Affleck). "Ethan approached her — he told her he was separated," said a source. In fact, one on-set source said that he and his wife couldn't even be in the same room together. Hawke and Perzow were even spotted at a Norah Jones concert that summer.

Thurman, while promoting her acclaimed work in *Kill Bill Vol. 1*, didn't want to talk about it. "I have two children, and I think it's the best way to deal with it," she told *GQ* in 2003. Hawke was more forthcoming: "You know, in a marriage, somebody's gotta ride shotgun," he told 20/20 in March. "If both people want to drive, keep fighting about who's gonna drive, you're gonna have a hard time. And eventually, you might have to say, "You know what? We gotta take two cars. You know, I don't know whether it's that I'm too much, you know, I got too much boy in me."

Jennifer Garner and Scott Foley

They seemed so wholesome. The couple — who met on the set of *Felicity* in 1998 and wed in October 2000 — proudly told reporters they like to cook, play Scrabble, and hang out with their two dogs, Maggie Mae and Charlie Rose, and cat, Wesley. "We're just a plain old married couple," she said. After the Golden Globes in 2002 (where she won Outstanding Actress in a Drama for the breakout hit *Alias*), they shunned the parties to eat a pizza at home. Imagine the shock when they announced on April 1, 2003, that they have mutually decided to separate.

But, in hindsight, there were signs of trouble. "It's hard right now spending time with each other," Foley, thirty-two, admitted in January. "It's stolen moments in the weekends at 3 A.M. when she comes in." Garner, thirty-two, as famous for her workaholism as for her flawless body, logged sixteen-hour days on the *Alias* set. "I don't think she has time for marriage," said a source.

Another factor was divergent career trajectories. When they met, Foley was, as he once called himself, "almost a household name," and Garner was a struggling actress. When they split, his sitcom, *AUSA*, was on hiatus while her star kept rising. "Their roles were reversed, and it was hard on Scott," said a source. "Scott did not want to be Mr. Jennifer Garner." Garner, however, understood the price of success: "It's hard to strike a balance between the fact that you're so grateful to have your job … and at the same time put yourself or your family first," she said months before the split. "I'm definitely learning about that."

Further complicating matters was speculation that her sexy *Alias* love interest, Michael Vartan, had become an off-screen love interest. "He's been in love with her for years," said a source. Vartan once said, "Our leading lady, Jennifer Garner, is hands-down fantastic on so many levels."

Indeed, in 2003, after Foley and Garner split, she and Vartan started up a real-life romance. They broke it off in the summer of 2004, and Garner went on to date Affleck. Foley has dated actress Marika Dominczyk for a year.

Tom Cruise & Nicole Kidman

Before Pitt and Aniston, there was Cruise and Kidman. They had captivated fans from the moment they hooked up in 1989 while filming *Days of Thunder*. "He took my breath away," said Kidman. "I don't know what it was — chemical reaction?" Cruise was a good-looking Hollywood heavyweight with hits like *Top Gun* and *Rain Man*; she was the exquisitely beautiful Australian-bred wife. They wed in a civil ceremony in December 1990. (Less than a year after he and actress Mimi Rogers were divorced). In January 1993, they adopted a daughter, Isabella; two years later, they adopted a son, Conor Anthony.

To hear them tell it, the marriage was one for the books. "I hope that when I am 80 years old ..." Kidman had said in 2000, "I am still married to the man that I fell in love with when I was 22." By all accounts, they were hopelessly romantic — during a night out in November 2000 at a New York City club, Kidman did a sexy dance for her husband, while he leaned against a wall, watched and enjoyed the show. They vowed to never spend more than three weeks apart at a time — even as her career grew with roles in 1995's *To Die For* and 2001's *Moulin Rouge!* On Christmas Eve, 2000, the couple, who also costarred in 1992's *Far and Away* and 1999's *Eyes Wide Shut*, even renewed their vows in their home before a gathering of close friends.

But they had their challenges. The couple often referred to themselves as "gypsies" who moved around constantly from their homes in Pacific Palisades, California; New York; and Sydney, Australia. "So much of who you are is where you grew up, and you want that to still be a part of your life," she has said. The couple turned inward, closing off intruders with confidentiality agreements, lawsuits (they successfully sued tabloids who claimed Cruise was gay and the marriage was a hoax); and, thus, become increasingly dependent on each other. As for their careers, Cruise reportedly wanted to keep his status as the go-to-leading-man in Hollywood (and develop his passion for producing), while Kidman longed to do plays, travel and take time off.

A little more than a month after their ten-year anniversary — and two weeks after they looked unusually glum at the Golden Globe Awards — their publicist issued a carefully worded statement announcing their separation. "They have regretfully decided to separate ... [They have] great respect for each other, both personally and professionally. Citing the difficulties inherent in divergent careers which constantly keep them apart, they concluded that an amicable separation seemed best for both of them at this time." Kidman reportedly did not see the announcement coming.

In the end, the inevitable pressure of their differences and their long-term goals proved too much. Of course, that didn't stop the hot gossip about a third party. Tabloids speculated that Kidman had rekindled a romance with Australian actor Marcus Graham. Then, months later, when Kidman suffered a miscarriage, there were whispers that the baby might not have been Cruise's. (She wound up filing documents, per Cruise's request, to confirm that he was the baby's father).

All along, they didn't hide from the public: Kidman lamented about the split while promoting *Moulin Rouge!* and *The Others* in 2001, but maintained an upbeat attitude. "Obviously, my children have a father who's going to be completely involved, but in terms of doing it alone, that's scary," she said in *Marie Claire*. "It's a whole new path I'm about to walk. And it's daunting." Cruise was equally optimistic, wishing "Nic" nothing but the best.

Four years later, the two have moved on: Cruise dated *Vanilla Sky* costar Penelope Cruz for almost three years; Kidman, who won a

Best Actress Oscar for *The Hours* in 2003, was briefly involved with Lenny Kravitz in late 2003 and she's now linked to billionaire producer Steve Bing. True to their separation statement, they remain close friends.

★ ★ ★

Like the hero he played in *Troy*, Pitt seemed ready to conquer any obstacles facing his own Hollywood marriage. "When it comes to anxiety, we balance each other out," he said in 2004. "But I'm a big believer in that it's the mistakes that define you as much as anything. It's there you get a real understanding of yourself [and] your partner. You can't have one without the other." Seconded Aniston, "We'll remind each other to trust in whatever the big picture is. There are certain things I'll get worked up about, like being hounded constantly, and want to be the one to change it, and he will ground me. It's a good balance."

Then again, Pitt was also aware of the reality of their union. As he told *Vanity Fair* in 2004, "Neither of us wants to be the spokesman for happy marriage, for coupledom."

CHAPTER 12

Family Matters

Staying married in Hollywood is enough of a challenge without factoring in an individual's own background. In the case of Pitt and Aniston, opposites attracted: He was a Midwesterner whose parents have been together for over forty years, she was a city kid with family dysfunction to spare. Was it too tough a match?

"I came from a very white-bread Christian community," Pitt told *Vanity Fair* of his hometown of Springfield, Missouri. "There were 1,800 students in my high school. Four were black." A preppy kid who played on the tennis team and sang in the church choir, the future star was the typical All-American boy, as popular among the students at Kickapoo High School as he was with their parents. "Brad was a great kid," said Bob Bilyou, a congregant at the South Haven Baptist Church, where Pitt (who was best friends with Bilyou's son Jody) sang in the choir.

Teen angst, it seemed, just wasn't part of young Brad's agenda. "He was a clean-living kid," Steve Fielding, his senior year tennis coach said. Indeed, after seeing *Raiders of the Lost Ark* with a date, the pair retreated to his parents' house where they ordered pizza and Pitt drank milk on ice. Added Fielding, "He was a fun kid, showed up to practice on time. He was very good-natured." His former math teacher, Jim Springston, got the same impression. "Everything about him is positive," he explained. "He was a top student, everyone liked him."

No doubt, much of the credit belongs to his still-married parents, Bill and Jane. "He came from a great family," said Bilyou. To this day, Brad is still close with them, as well as his brother, Doug, who owns a computer business, and sister Julie Neal, a married, stay-at-home mom. (Brad is three years older than Doug, who is two years older than Julie; in 2004, they both appeared as coffee-drinking extras on *Friends*.) Despite his fame and fortune, the actor has held on to his down-home Midwestern values. "I don't want to be a part of some egomaniac train I'm leading," he told a British paper. "I want to have a good time and hang out with people and have a laugh. Really, that's it. That's me. I come from a very humble background and I lived that life a lot longer than I've lived some Hollywood life." And if, by chance, he forgets that, his family is there to keep him in check. "We all abuse him tremendously," joked Bill. "Nobody cuts him any slack."

To his future wife, Pitt's childhood must have sounded foreign. After stints in Sherman Oaks, California, and Greece, her family settled in New York City, where her father worked as an actor. Before her parents divorced when she was nine, the Aniston household was an entertaining place to be. "My favorite memory is when they would have poker parties," she recalled to Diane Sawyer, "'cause my dad is, was and still is on a soap opera. And their actor friends would come and sing songs around the piano and play games, play — play charades. And they were just funny, fun people." If her Greek relatives were around, Aniston would sometimes thrill the adults by belly dancing. "I used to cut a real mean one," she told *Esquire*.

The good times ended when her father, John, suddenly left her mother, Nancy, for another woman. "It was quick," the actress told Sawyer. "There one minute and, boom. Yeah. I think it was like ripping off a band-aid, probably easier that way ... So, it was pretty quick." The impact, meanwhile, was long-lasting. As the star explained in 1997, "I want to get married someday, but I guess I'm sort of cautious. My parents' divorce makes me very aware of what to look for in a partner and who to trust."

It was a year before Aniston communicated with her father again. And then, being stuck in the middle of her parents' fractured relationship was not an easy place for a little girl to be. "I learned a lot about human relations and emotions at a young age, dealing with adults who were all of a sudden children," she explained. "It's definitely hard. You deal with them fighting through you. That's a drag."

Seeming to take a cue from *The Parent Trap*, Aniston schemed to get the couple back together by behaving badly at school. "When I got in trouble, my mom and dad would have to meet in the principal's office," she told *Esquire*. "There was *that* little manipulation for a while. But it didn't work out. It's hard to impress your dad when you're in the principal's office for being stupid." If anything positive came out of this period, it was her comedic talents. "I was always the mediator," she explained. "I was always trying to smooth things over and get everyone to laugh."

Though he was an actor, John never encouraged his daughter to follow in his footsteps. "It's not the kind of business anybody would wish on their child," he said in 1997. "It's fine if it goes the way it has gone for her, but if not, it can be devastating." Still, that didn't stop him from landing her a bit part on the soap opera *Search for Tomorrow* when she was thirteen. "I remember sitting at a table right behind where the main actors were," she said, recalling the scene in which she played an ice skater and wore a yellow dress. "And they couldn't see me, so they had one of the other kids and I change places. I got special treatment because I was Daddy's Girl."

At the time, she felt embarrassed and angry, but two years later, she used her father's connections to her advantage. Secretly, Aniston (whose godfather, actor Telly Savalas, encouraged her to pursue acting) rang up her dad's agent to ask him to get her an audition for a movie role. Years later, the elder Aniston finally came around, and he even brought her the script to the 1997 movie *Picture Perfect*. "My dad knows what's up and he's a pretty extraordinary man," she said.

But it's Aniston's relationship with Nancy that has truly complicated her life. There was the usual mother-daughter stuff, of course, like comments on teenage Jennifer's physical appearance. But into the actress' early adulthood, they were extremely close.

"When I was growing up, she and I were so connected," the actress told *O*. She once described Nancy as "very warm, loving, nurturing, wise, funny, and old-fashioned. And when it got rough out there, in terms of the career, she was the one who said keep going, keep going."

When the actress moved to L.A. and created another "family" made up of her newfound friends, Nancy (and others) felt hurt. "It was hard for them to understand these other people always being there — my mother especially," Aniston revealed in British *Elle*. "I know she puts my life down a lot. She didn't understand how special and protective these people were. If only she knew, I think she would have felt less threatened and embraced them."

The relationship really hit the skids, however, in 1996, when Nancy (who lives in North Hollywood, a little more than ten miles from Aniston's Beverly Hills home) discussed her daughter's childhood on the tabloid TV show *Hard Copy*. At that point, Aniston stopped speaking to her mother; and as Nancy later recalled, called her on the phone and yelled, "I'll never forgive you!" In 1999, Nancy published the memoir *From Mother and Daughter to Friends: A Memoir*, which only deepened their rift. (Aniston has never read the book.) Critics wondered how she could do such a thing in light of her daughter's anger, but she explained, "I'm a writer. It's a book about me. It's just a coincidence that I have a celebrity daughter." The timing of the fallout meant that Nancy never met Pitt. "My husband doesn't know my mother," noted Aniston in *Vogue*, "and that's weird, because she was my life."

Coping with the estrangement has been difficult for the actress. "Lord knows, I wish I had a different situation with my mom," she told *Esquire*. "You know something, lots of daughters have difficult relationships with their mothers. Only when you're under a microscope, it gets played out in public like it's some kind of court trial. You walk out of your therapist's office — he works out of his house in a quiet neighborhood — and there are four vans with lenses popping out."

Still, she did speak about the relationship in many interviews over the years, and didn't rule out a reconciliation. "It's just a matter of time," she said in *W* in 2003. She added, "I don't need an apology because I already know the truth, and if I approach her with an expectation of an apology it could just lead to disappointment. I just, at some point I'll just have to let go and decide to forgive her, which I can't do yet."

A year later, a reunion of the Aniston women still had not happened. "A lot of me is being very stubborn and very self-righteous in my position of how I was wronged by my mom," Aniston confessed to *Vogue*. "And I think there comes a point where you have to grow up and get over yourself, lighten up … and forgive. People are who they are and they make mistakes. I definitely see that there's hope." In fact, she added, "I look in the mirror, I watch [*Friends*], and I'm like, 'Oh, my God. You're Nancy.' You've become her, so you may as well call her."

Nancy's friends feel sorry for the star's mother. "She's heartbroken," said a pal. "What does she have to look forward to — not being able to see her grandchildren?" Added the source, "Nancy will tell you, 'Read my book. Tell me if there is one thing in it that would cause all of this.'" Beverly Hills Realtor Elaine Young, a longtime pal of the elder Aniston, hoped for a reunion. "Nancy is the sweetest, nicest, person, and what has happened is terrible, I really feel for her," she said. "If she talks to the press, if she doesn't talk, nothing seems to be working. They need to make up, put this behind them and move on with their lives for both their sakes."

Even in the silence, Nancy has provided inspiration for her daughter. When the actress took on the role of Justine, the lonely, small-town wife in *The Good Girl*, she felt a connection to her mother. "Justine was so beautifully written that there wasn't much to do except fall into character," she explained to a British paper, "but my mom did come into my head because I've always thought of her as someone who's getting to the end of her life and didn't get to do what she wanted to do."

Could Aniston's strained relationship with her mother have led to her strained relationship with Pitt? "My guess is she's very mistrustful of relationships and permanence," noted Michele Weiner-Davis, creator of Divorcebusting.com. One source close to the couple had another theory. "I am not Freud, but I think the fact that Aniston has had such a bad relationship with her mother is a big part of this," the source said. "My sense is she is so scarred from her own mother-daughter thing that she can't bear the thought of having it repeat itself [by having children with Pitt]."

For her part, Aniston predicted having a baby would have helped her with her issues. "I'm sure when I have my own child it will help heal some of these things," she told *Allure* in 2004 of the relationship with her mother. "But I can't even put my mind around that right now. But children, yes, always provide healing. They provide clarity."

CHAPTER 13

The Third Year's a Charm

Only one month into 2003 and Aniston and Pitt had already wrung their hands of a year's worth of gossip and whispers about their marriage.

But if the couple was affected, they didn't let it show. Besides, there was a birthday coming up — Aniston's thirty-fourth on February 11 — and the two never disappointed when it came to celebrating each other's special day. This year, Pitt was in luck: His wife was already on location in the ultra-romantic setting of Honolulu filming the comedy *Along Came Polly* with Ben Stiller and Hank Azaria.

The actor took a private plane to Hawaii and met up with Aniston for almost a week of fun in the sun. One night, he joined her and her cast mates for a dinner at Hale'iwa Joe's (locals still buzzed about the evening weeks later). On February 11, he threw a lavish party for Aniston and about 100 friends on the Bay View Beach of the ritzy Turtle Bay Resort. The affair featured fire knife dancers, pupu prepared by the hotel, a sheet of chocolate cake from Dee Lite Bakery, and many mai tais. His gift to her? A band of small, delicate diamonds that Aniston wore above her wedding ring.

Ah, yes, all was well. Back home later that month the couple was spotted on a double date with Warren Beatty and Annette Bening at the upscale French restaurant L'Orangerie in West Hollywood. In good spirits, the couple joked with the waiters and shared a chocolate soufflé for dessert. In March, they breezily made the scene at the Independent Spirit Awards, where Aniston was nominated for her role in *The Good Girl* (an Oscar nomination, however, was not in the cards). An onlooker said Pitt gently touched the small of her back on the red carpet as she hurriedly made her way through the line — and even watched her saunter out again on the way to the bathroom. The two were all smiles again in April at Friends for a Cure ALS benefit in Los Angeles, as they held hands on the red carpet.

By the end of April, however, the couple faced the longest separation of their nearly three-year marriage. After almost twelve months of physical training, Pitt headed to Malta to start filming his role as Achilles in *Troy*— his first movie in nearly two years. "It's hard," Aniston said in May 2003 of the long-distance factor. "He goes away on a lot of his movies. It's a weird thing that we [actors] do — we have to leave our spouses. We've been lucky because [since we've been married], he's only had *Spy Game* and that was for a short period of time. [But] this is a huge movie epic, so it's different."

No doubt, Aniston was even more agitated over Pitt's workload when she headed back to Hawaii on May 1 to attend the romantic and intimate wedding of cast mate Matt LeBlanc and his longtime fiancée, Melissa McKnight. Though by all accounts she enjoyed her weekend in paradise (especially when she and Cox drank margaritas, ate nachos, and laid out on the beach the day before LeBlanc's wedding), Aniston was still stuck being a third wheel.

Soon, Aniston and Pitt announced a new joint production. Despite rising expectations, it was not baby news. Instead, as partners of the new Plan B production company, they decided to coproduce an upcoming film based on the best-selling novel *The Time Traveler's Wife*.

As for the baby talk, Aniston declared that the couple would try "once *Friends* is finished." But her career had just started to heat up — *Bruce Almighty* was released on May 23, and though Aniston was second-billed to Jim

Carrey, it was the biggest movie blockbuster of her career. "I'm not somebody who has mapped out my career or my life and said, 'by this time, I want to do this.' There are things that, in hindsight, I might not have done, but I still had a great experience with every job I've had, it's all part of the building blocks of who I am." Tellingly, she had also added: "I would go crazy if I didn't work. I came from a place with no money."

Aniston did not stick around Hollywood to bask in the success of *Bruce Almighty*. On May 24, the fearful flier — she wore a St. Christopher medallion for travel — headed 6,500 miles to the Mediterranean island of Malta to join her husband on location. "Let me tell you something, that ain't no short trip," she later told *Vogue*. Though tabloids reported that Aniston came to the set because she was bothered by Pitt's relationship with his costar, German model Diane Kruger, Aniston scoffed at the notion: "I had a period in my life when I was younger when I was jealous, but I don't feel that now. He's very loyal; he's not impressed with that sort of stuff. So thankfully I'm not a model!"

For a week, the couple cozied up like newlyweds at the island's top restaurants, including the five-star Xara Palace in Mdina, where a fellow diner said that they held each other's hands across the table all night. When they weren't out and about, the pair holed up at the their rented villa in Bahar Ic-Caghaq, complete with a pool, Jacuzzi, steam room, and private driveway with 24-hour security. They also took advantage of the horses and paddock on the estate's grounds, where Pitt practiced riding. By the time their romantic week ended, a local tour guide said, "Jennifer liked it so much she said they were thinking of buying a house here."

Still, there's no place like home. Pitt returned to Los Angeles on July 10. The very next day, the two enjoyed a romantic lunch at Balboa Restaurant & Lounge in West Hollywood — where they shared a toast. Aniston had just received her fourth Emmy nomination and topped the latest *Forbes* Celebrity 100 list.

Pitt's stay in L.A. was short-lived, however. A few days later, he headed to Mexico to continue his work on *Troy*. But the couple was determined to be together. "We just call it by [saying] 'I got an itch,' you know?" Pitt explained. The couple turned the shoot into a sexy getaway — their third anniversary was on the horizon, after all. The pair set up camp in a deluxe villa on a seaside cliff in the gated community El Pedregal (which featured sun decks, a pool, and an outdoor gym). On July 22, husband and wife shared a quiet dinner on their patio. The following weekend, Aniston and Pitt hit the beach for a day of sunning. "She came and we had a good, nice week together," Pitt added.

The third-year honeymoon ended in August, when Aniston headed back to L.A. to start filming the tenth and final season of *Friends*. Indeed, with Pitt hundreds of miles away, Aniston got by with a little help from her pals. On September 20, she went (stag) to the nuptials of Melissa Etheridge and Tammy Lynn Michaels, where she danced past midnight. The next day, the actress showed up to the Emmy Awards hand-in-hand with her matron of honor, Andrea Bendewald. (Turned out, Aniston needed the support: She lost out to her *Along Came Polly* costar Debra Messing).

At the post-awards *Friends* party at Spago, Aniston and Bendewald made a beeline for the food buffet, where they filled up on identical plates of Caesar salad, chicken in mushroom sauce, mashed potatoes, and tortellini filled with cheese. "I got your silverware!" Aniston said to her pal, as they joined Lisa Kudrow and Christina Applegate at a table. Later, Aniston kissed and hugged Applegate before grabbing Bendewald's hand and leaving at 11 P.M.

Finally, in October, production on *Troy* wrapped after a brutal five-month schedule. To celebrate, the reunited couple went to dinner with Cox and Arquette at Spago (they arrived in their new Toyota Hybrid). The timing couldn't have been better to have her biggest fan nearby — Aniston was nearing the wrap date of *Friends*. "It's going to tear me apart to say goodbye," she said. "It's been a part of me for so long, I can't even imagine it. ," also adding, "It's better to go out with people still loving us."

Still, Aniston had big plans for her post-*Friends* life: "I'm about to go somewhere and I don't know where yet," she said. "We haven't been on a vacation in about two years — not since we had our first anniversary. There are a lot of places I haven't been to. I still have a lot of traveling to do." And when prodded on the baby issue, "I'm very excited about [having a baby]. I think when *Friends* is finished it's the time. I hope that chapter of life will be done with. Having kids will probably be our next job."

But by the end of 2003, Aniston's immediate job was figuring out how to properly celebrate Pitt's upcoming milestone — his fortieth birthday on December 18. Pitt, for one, eagerly anticipated the occasion (even though he had to film some extra fight scenes for *Troy* during the afternoon). "I see it as a real badge of honor," he said. "I enjoyed it. No more excuses, you know? I'm responsible. I can't blame anything on my parents. I'm responsible for my mistakes and my choices."

Aniston cooked up something extra special: Jetting their favorite chef Jamie Oliver (and his wife, Jools) from England to L.A. to prepare a private dinner. She also presented him with a huge Russell Young-designed silkscreen on canvas of Pitt's all-time idol, *The Great Escape* actor Steve McQueen, taken from a 1972 police mug shot. (Young, an L.A.-based artist whose works are reminiscent of Andy Warhol, also has paid tribute to such scandalous stars as Frank Sinatra, Sid Vicious, Charles Manson, Jane Fonda, and Patty Hearst). The estimated cost: $10,000–15,000.

For Pitt it was the perfect way to commemorate his day: "I'd always said I was going to get something like a Rolls Royce for my birthday.

But then I got into energy conservation. Instead, I got back [from the *Troy* set] and had a quiet dinner with my friends and my wife. It was a nice little dinner at home."

Their busy year finished with a flourish. The *New York Post* reported the couple attended a costume party and dressed up by paying tribute to each other. Aniston looked like Helen of Troy, in a nod to her husband's upcoming sandal epic. As for Pitt, he did his best eighties imitation and transformed himself — eye makeup and all — into Duran Duran lead singer Simon Le Bon, his wife's childhood celebrity crush. Pitt reportedly even warbled a karaoke version of the band's 1985 hit, "Wild Boys." Onlookers said Aniston couldn't stop smiling all night, as Pitt made her fanzine dreams come true.

Certainly, the fun-filled evening was a contrast to the couple's sour demeanor at the start of 2003. They had put the marriage-on-the-rocks rumor to bed. For the time being, at least.

CHAPTER 14

Inside Their Style

Over the course of their marriage, Aniston and Pitt just seemed to get more and more good looking. From their hair to their wardrobes, there was rarely a misstep (let's forget about the time in 2002 when Pitt grew long hair and a mountain man beard). On the red carpet, they were the picture of understated elegance; in their every day lives, California cool. For their wedding day in July 2000, Pitt and Aniston — Hollywood's best-tressed twosome — had even sported matching sun-kissed highlights, courtesy of colorist Michael Canale of the Canale Salon in Beverly Hills.

But odds are Aniston wouldn't have become such a style setter if it weren't for "The Rachel." In 1995, towards the end of the first season of *Friends*, her hairstylist Chris McMillan wanted to help the actress grow out her bangs, and give her a cut that would "look like today but a little hipper." Little did he know, those few snips would turn her into a household name, and set off a hair trend that has been compared to the Farrah Fawcett-inspired craze of the 1970s.

Aniston has been trying to live it down ever since. "She was becoming known for a head of hair," said colorist Canale. "That consumed her." To make matters worse, Aniston wasn't even a fan of the look. "All I have to say about that is, 'What the hell was I thinking?' I had dead, trashed, burnt hair — they ironed it so much for the show," she told W in 1999.

In the years that followed, the natural brunette grew her hair long, added blonde highlights, wore it wavy, added extensions, chopped it off, cut bangs — and despite what *she* may have thought, it always looked good. "I've hated my hair all my life," she said in 1997. "It's always been curly, and I wanted it straight. I've tried to do everything I could to have control over it in some way. So all of a sudden to have that [Rachel phenomenon] happen was bizarre."

In 2001, Aniston tried to make a fresh start by getting a bob. Years later, she confessed it was a "dumb-ass move." But perhaps not as dumb as having a mohawk, or coloring her hair black or with Clairol Boysenberry dye, both of which she did during high school. "It was magenta," the once-rebellious teen admitted to a magazine in 2004, "I don't know how to explain it." (Suffice it to say, it went with her heavy applications of liquid eyeliner.) A better moment was when she arrived at the Golden Globes in 2003 with her hair looking noticeably darker than it had been in years. As a rule, explained Canale, "Jen does not like to look 'done.'"

For a guy, Pitt had a fair share of hair moments — a few of which happened to coincide with his wife's. In addition to the his-and-hers wedding highlights, there were the cropped tops of 2001 with her bob and his *Ocean's Eleven* crew cut, and the joint long-layered looks of 2003 when he returned from the set of *Troy*. According to media-psychology expert Stuart Fischoff, loving couples "tend to become like each other. They want to become one."

At times, Aniston even acted as Pitt's personal groomer, cutting his hair and shaving his beard. This type of work was nothing new for the actress: In high school, "she really liked to do people's hair," recalled a classmate. "She was into hair cutting and we would talk about hairstyles." Fast-forward to almost twenty years later, and nothing has changed. "I'm a closet hairdresser," she admitted. "I've even done my girlfriends' hair for weddings. I figure I have something to fall back on."

In return, Pitt would offer his wife fashion advice. "My husband taught me about clothes," she revealed in O in 2004. "He'd say, 'You can't put those two materials together,' and I'd be like, 'I've been doing this for years.'" During his tenure at Springfield, Missouri's Kickapoo High School, he was voted best dressed, thus leading to his style maven status. Kickapoo alum Monica Blades remembered, "He wore Izods — pink and purple were really big — with knit ties."

Today, Pitt, who once appeared in an ad for Levis 501 jeans, can often be found in a T-shirt and shorts or jeans. (Oddly, in 2002, he was spotted in a series of T-shirts bearing the number "7"; in 2004, the word "Trash" was printed across his chest.) When it's time to dress up Pitt favors slim suits by Prada or Hedi Slimane, in addition to Giorgio Armani, Richard Tyler, and Calvin Klein.

As a teenager in New York City, Aniston's wardrobe wasn't as colorful or preppy. "I was always the girl who wore the big black skirts because I was a little chunkier and that's all I could wear," she recalled in Harper's Bazaar. Bendewald, however, referred to her as "very chic." And another school mate said, "As far as I remember her, she was very stylish. I don't remember her being a total fashion plate, but she certainly was well dressed. She was certainly into fashion. I remember we would talk about where to find the perfect boots."

These days, she doesn't have to look further than her closet, which is filled with clothes from top designers. Her favorites include Marc Jacobs ("he's comfortable"), and Ralph Lauren, and Calvin Klein ("I love that in their clothes, the body is what stands out, the person"). And she can't do without her high heels. "I am a shoe fanatic," she said in *Bazaar*. At five-foot-five, the actress called herself "a bit of a shrimp, so anytime I can look a little taller, I'm happy." As for fashion, "I love it," she said. "I love when people put me in it. And God knows, I'm slowly getting better at putting stuff together myself."

But if it were up to her, Aniston — who hates lace and pink — would only wear "safe" and comfy staples like khakis or cargo pants, fitted tank tops or cozy T-shirts, and sandals or sneakers. "When we pick a restaurant, my criteria is, 'Can I wear this?' " she once said. Though she claimed she didn't "get" fashion, in recent years she has come around. "I try to stay up on it," she confessed, "but I just don't like being ruled by it." Plus, she has said that it's no fun putting on something fashionable that makes it difficult to breathe. "I'm more comfortable in a simple dress I can just wear and kick off my shoes and sit cross-legged on the couch," she told one magazine.

But just because Aniston looks like she shops at the Gap, that doesn't mean her clothes carry Gap prices. Once she marveled at how she much she had spent on a vintage Mickey Mouse T-shirt. "I never knew I could pay $170 for an old, old T-shirt that somebody else wore," she admitted to *Bazaar*. "And I paid for it, willingly!"

Because she's so laid-back, the actress usually shies away from using a professional stylist when it's time to dress up for a big night out. "I get too overwhelmed with a stylist, and the whole deal can feel contrived," she explained to the fashion magazine. "Half of the time I'll pair a piece from my own closet, like an old T-shirt with something like a fabulous pair of Gucci pants."

Aniston also knows how to turn it on when she strolls the red carpet. Some of her most memorable fashion hits: the peach chiffon Christian Dior gown that she wore when she won an Emmy Award in 2002. "She wore that dress with the ease of a girl wearing a pair of jeans," Dior designer John Galliano said. The actress followed up in 2003 with a short, navy blue vintage Halston dress. Halston designer Bradley Bayou explained that the star had a "girlie flirtatiousness, but there's also elegance." Her choice that year not only was a refreshing change of pace in a sea of floor-length gowns, but it was also a departure for Aniston. "I've never worn a vintage dress," she admitted in *Vogue*. "I just had the urge. I wasn't feeling gowny and fabulous. I just wasn't in that mood. I waited till the last minute, as usual, and I found that beautiful dress. Didn't even have to have it altered."

At the 2004 Golden Globes, she chose vintage again, and wowed the crowd in a black Valentino gown with a plunging, buckle-accented neckline. She made a splash in a classic strapless red Valentino gown the following month at the *Along Came Polly* premiere in London, but Aniston's defining dresses of 2004 were both white: First, a halter-neck, beaded Atelier Versace gown that she wore at the Cannes Film Festival. Standing next to Pitt, the couple never looked happier or more perfect. Then, at the Emmy Awards, a strapless

Chanel column that she dubbed "a little bo-hemian." (Sadly, it was the last time the pic-ture perfect couple would make a red carpet appearance together.) Explained stylist Rachel Zoe, "She opts for elegant, timeless looks."

To be fair, Aniston has made some fashion mistakes. "A couple of outfits I've worn were pointed out," she noted to *Bazaar*. "One was just black pants paired with a black shirt. How do you screw that up? Somehow I did... . And once I was told that a jacket I'd worn looked like a lab coat, which it did." Looking back at the cleavage-baring Dolce & Gabbana number that she wore to NBC's 75th Anniversary cele-bration in 2002, she called the evening "my Dolly Parton night." But none of those blun-ders compare to the glittering Halston dress she wore to the 1999 Emmy Awards. (She also had dreadlocks that night.) Afterward, Aniston found herself on Mr. Blackwell's worst-dressed list. Though she has called the gown "beauti-ful," she has also admitted that it "looked like I'd come right off the set of *Dynasty*. I never got more ripped to pieces."

So which stars does Aniston think have great style? "Obviously Gwyneth Paltrow is fashion-perfect," she said in a surprising nod to Pitt's ex-fiancée in *Bazaar*. "And Kate Hudson and Cameron Diaz. They really do have a knack for putting things together and looking great. I admire women who can do that."

She also has a lot of respect for people who have the courage to attend fashion shows. In 2001, Pitt and Aniston checked out a Giorgio Armani show in Milan; naturally, the couple — who wore coordinating beige ensembles — sat in the front row, but it didn't matter to her. "I went to one show and that was enough for me," she said. "I always leave those things feeling bad, somehow. I feel like a bit of an outsider." She explained another time, "If I have to go and look at clothes, I'll go to a store."

The fact is, Pitt and Aniston don't need to steal ideas from the catwalk. They have done fine on their own, according to experts.

"She exudes an energy that is sexy and wholesome at the same time," *Friends* wardrobe designer Debra Maguire said in 2001. "She really understands her body in terms of what looks great." As for Pitt, designer Pamela Dennis has said the man can basically do anything. "He pulls off Prada, three-piece suits, and leather and jeans and cargo pants. I don't think he could go wrong."

CHAPTER 15

Baby Talk

It's a math problem for the ages: Does one handsome man plus one gorgeous woman equal one beautiful baby?

This was the thought on everyone's mind almost as soon as Pitt and Aniston wed, and anticipation grew over the course of the marriage as the pair spoke openly about their desire to start a family. Even as pregnancy rumors swirled, Aniston seemed to take it all in stride. "I found it hysterical," she said.

Still, no one would have made such an issue out of their future children if the couple didn't make such an issue out of it themselves. As far back as 1997, the actress discussed how much she liked babies, and even hinted at a timetable for motherhood. "I love everything about them," she gushed to *Cosmopolitan*. "Their backs, necks, smell, all their fits. I want to be a young mom, too. I'm not ready now, but in a couple of years …"

According to a source close to Pitt, "Brad wanted a family from the time they got married." Actually, not just a family, but what he called "a commune" — seven kids, to be exact. Sure, Aniston once acknowledged, "I was born with the hips to make [babies]," but she was thinking a bit smaller. Eventually, the number was whittled down to "two, at least. [A] brother and sister," she revealed in 2004.

In 2001, the baby talk geared up. "I believe in the concept of marriage and family, and it has always been my intention to take this step and build a life with someone," Pitt told a British newspaper. "Planning is under way; negotiations are taking place; and I'm willing to predict a successful conclusion." The following year, when Aniston believed she was on her last season of *Friends*, she explained why she didn't want the sitcom to continue by saying, "I want to start my family." She even went so far as to say she was "absolutely" ready to take time off to be a mom.

But Aniston's intentions seemed to drift as her career took off. Each time she renewed her contract for *Friends* was another year parenthood would have to wait. "We had a window there when Rachel was pregnant on the show [in 2001–2002 season]; it would have been great, but we were doing other things," she said to *Harper's Bazaar* in 2003. But that same year she also admitted, "It's something we are definitely thinking about. I'm very excited about that." Though they had no due date in sight, the couple carried on like potential parents-to-be and built the nursery in their Beverly Hills home.

Had Aniston become pregnant while her sitcom was still on the air, it really wouldn't have been a problem. "Lisa [Kudrow] had a baby during the show," David Arquette said of the *Friends* costar, whose own pregnancy was written into the series in 1998 — albeit as surrogate triplets. "It can easily be done," he added. Plenty of other TV actresses — including *Will & Grace*'s Debra Messing, *Everybody Loves Raymond*'s Patricia Heaton, and *Sex and the City*'s Sarah Jessica Parker — have also hidden their expanding bumps behind pillows, shopping bags, and loose fitting tops. In fact, during the final season of *Friends*, Courteney Cox joined the club.

As it was, Aniston already had plenty of experience playing a mother on film and television. When Rachel was pregnant on *Friends*, she reportedly read pregnancy books on set. In 2002's *The Good Girl*, her character had a baby, and in the 2003 hit *Bruce Almighty*, she played a nurturing kindergarten teacher. Even as far back as 1997, she got a taste of pregnancy: In the comedy *Object of My Affection*, she played a single mother who falls in love with her gay best friend (played by future *Friends* recurring guest star Paul Rudd). For part of the movie, the actress wore a fake pregnancy belly. "I can only hope that I feel this good when it's my turn to actually carry a baby," she said while shooting the film.

There was never any mention of whether Aniston might have had trouble conceiving (like best friend Courteney Cox), but she did wear a fertility medallion around her neck. Certainly, as a woman in her thirties, she heard her biological clock ticking. "I'd love to procreate sooner rather than later," she said in 2003, "so that I'm not a grandmother and mother at the same time." According to Pamela Madsen, the executive director of the American Infertility Association, a woman's fertility significantly declines after the age of thirty-five. "If they want a little Pitt, the best chance to do it is now," Madsen said in 2003. Beverly Hills fertility specialist Dr. Arthur Wisot, coauthor of *Conceptions & Misconceptions*, said the decrease is more significant at age thirty-eight, but also suggested that a woman like Aniston make motherhood a priority. "Put the movies off," he advised. "Your ovaries don't care how great you look or how much you exercise. At some point, you start not producing healthy eggs." If she did have any trouble, costar and pal Matthew Perry graciously (and jokingly) offered his support. "If she and Brad need any help, I'll swing by," the actor has said.

Even more troubling, though, was Aniston's smoking habit. The fact that she continued to puff away while she said she was going to start a family was a clear example of actions speaking louder than words. "Smoking and pregnancy are enemies," said Wisot. "When you smoke, you are taking in a huge amount of toxins that can adversely affect the reproductive process. It is clear that smoking adversely affects your chances of getting pregnant." The couple was well aware of that fact as far back as August 2002. "We do want to have a baby," she said when asked about a rumor that she and Pitt had given up cigarettes in preparation for parenthood. "We will eventually quit smoking."

Subconsciously, Aniston's estranged relationship with her own mother could have been one thing holding her back from becoming one herself. "When there are cutoffs in the family or breaks in important relationships, a woman often doesn't feel sufficiently rooted or stable enough to have a baby," explained psychologist and family therapist Dr. Florence Kaslow. Looking in the mirror, though, Aniston did see qualities that would make her a suitable parent. "I am patient," she said. "I am a nurturer — to a fault."

Indeed, no one ever doubted that both Pitt and Aniston *liked* children. "Jen really loves babies," said longtime pal Kristin Hahn. "She's a real softie for them." Pitt, meanwhile, doted on his nieces and nephews in Missouri. "He's their personal play gym. They climb all over him," younger brother Doug said. Their younger sister Julie acknowledged, "He hates to have his hair brushed, but he lets those girls brush his hair, and put makeup on him and nail polish on his fingernails and toenails. He is crazy mad about them." Such trips home, said a source close to Pitt, only increased the actor's desire to start his own family. After a trip there in 2004, an L.A.-based producer who knows the actor said, "I think when he left there, he probably had more of a longing for kids. Brad looks at his brother and his lifestyle and his kids and really admires him for it."

Some suspect Pitt's baby lust grew even

more while he was on the set of *Mr. and Mrs. Smith*. His costar Angelina Jolie brought her adopted two-year-old son Maddox to work, and the actor got a kick out of the little boy. "From the way Brad looked at him, you could tell he can't wait to have kids of his own," reported a witness. At one point, the actor sat on the grass and watched the tyke laugh and play with local kids.

By November 2003, Aniston gave the impression she felt the same way. During an *Oprah* interview with her cast mates she acknowledged, "I think the opportunity just hasn't really presented itself. I mean, there is that weird little knock and itching thing that does start to happen as you enter into your 30s." She continued, "I'm itching a little bit, yeah. Like I'll take a puppy that I see and just devour it. I mean like any little thing, you know. Even little Mattie [Matt LeBlanc] sometimes... I mean, definitely, it's that time... On to the next chapter."

Up until the sitcom wrapped in 2004, it seemed "When *Friends* is finished" was the couple's mantra. But early in the year, there were signs the couple was no longer on the same page. During an interview in January 2004 with Diane Sawyer, Aniston, the same person who once said, "You can have the baby on one arm and the script on another," seemed less inclined to attempt the balancing act. "[Parenthood] deserves time like my career deserves time," she now said. And by the amount of film roles she was racking up (by the end of the year, she had finished or signed on to a half dozen), it appeared she was going to continue to give her career top priority. Still, she told Sawyer, "This will probably be the most important job I'll ever do, having a baby."

In April, months after the final episode of *Friends* was taped, Pitt remarked, "Yeah, it's time. I finally think I'm at the place where I won't mess them up too much." Was Aniston in agreement, asked a reporter? "Jen's in agreement that I won't mess them up too much," he said cryptically. In early May, however, he backpedaled a bit and told Oprah Winfrey, "We're still in rehearsals. It's going very well, and I am excited about the future." As for his own preparedness, he was confident he'd make a great father. "I finally feel like I've got my stuff together where I'm ready for that… I'd be good at it."

The same week, during an interview with Katie Couric and Matt Lauer, Aniston (who had admitted she was taking folic acid, a supplement that prevents birth defects) said she needed more time. "The first thing I'm going to do is take a vacation," she explained. "I'm going to see as much of the world as I can before I have a child. And then it's — and then it's about family." Curiously, she told another media outlet around that time, "We're absolutely in the process [of having a baby]. It's where we're headed."

All of this must have been difficult and confusing for her husband, considering he had been so patient. Said a source close to the actor, "Jen was the one who wanted to wait. He thought if he gave her more time, let *Friends* finish, she would be ready."

By August, there was even talk that the couple was going to adopt. A British weekly cited the source as Doug Pitt, but he quickly announced the claim was bogus. "The story was 100 percent fabricated," he said. "I never did that interview." Pitt's rep added, "It's completely not true."

In the end, perhaps Pitt's longings proved too strong for the pair. And ultimately, the world will never know what Pitt and Aniston's beautiful children would have looked like. "Brad wants to be a dad more than anything," says a source close to Pitt. "Jen wants to do movies — she doesn't want to be Rachel Green forever. Brad finally realizes that she just doesn't want to be a mom — not now, maybe never."

CHAPTER 16

The Ups and Downs of 2004

As Pitt and Aniston rang in 2004, a few things were certain: The end of *Friends*; the May release of the $170-million epic *Troy*; a fourth-anniversary celebration in July. But who could have ever guessed that 2004 would also be their last year together as man and wife?

The year started off as hectic as ever. In January, Aniston had to deal with the simultaneous release of the comedy *Along Came Polly* and the wrap date of *Friends*. "I'm just hoping I get through the night," Aniston told Diane Sawyer, days before she sipped her last on-set latte. "I should have a shock thing around my neck like those dogs, when they start to bark. When I start to cry, I just get electrocuted."

On January 10, Aniston let off a little steam by hosting *Saturday Night Live*. The show was ultimately a 90-minute glimpse into her life. In one sketch, she played a nosy paparazzi photographer on an awards show red carpet who berated 'Jennifer Aniston' with the all-too-familiar question, "*When are you going to have a baby?*" More endearingly, during the closing moments of the show, Aniston came on stage sporting a white T-shirt emblazoned with the sentence "I Love Brad Pitt." She proved it two nights later when she and Pitt beamed on the red carpet for the Los Angeles premiere of *Along Came Polly*.

With dueling schedules, the couple tried to spend as much time as they could together. During Aniston's "free time," she often visited Pitt on the set of *Mr. and Mrs. Smith*, his new movie in which he and Angelina Jolie played married assassins (another source, however, insisted Aniston never dropped by). And though Pitt couldn't squeeze in the hours to watch the taping of the last *Friends* episode on January 23, he joined his wife for the wrap party extravaganza at Il Sole.

But they didn't stay in the same Beverly Hills zip code for long, which would prove to be a major theme for the rest of the year. In February, Aniston had to travel overseas to promote *Along Came Polly*, which became a big hit (despite scathing reviews) in the U.S. It was an exciting European jaunt — she and costar Ben Stiller toured the Musee d'Orsay and cruised the Seine in Paris. But Aniston was an ocean away from Pitt on her thirty-fifth birthday. And on Valentine's Day, she spent the night at the Berlin film premiere, while Pitt worked on his new movie — and bonded with Jolie and her little boy, Maddox.

In fact, Pitt was so busy on the film, he didn't even have time to escort Aniston to the Night Before the Oscars party on February 28. (Once again, she tagged along with Cox and Arquette). Aniston's explanation for Pitt's absence? "He's busy, and I just wanted to hang out with my friends." Cox and Arquette proved to be the perfect dates as they watched over her and took her home.

Aniston, meanwhile, was filling up her plate with projects. She inked a deal to star in a comedy, in which she'd play a woman who learns that her family may be the real-life inspiration for *The Graduate*. On March 29, it was announced the actress had signed on for a lead role in the crime caper *Gambit*. So much for the baby plans.

The couple went weeks without appearing together, as Aniston was spotted dining more often with her *Friends* cast mates than her husband, like the time Aniston dined with LeBlanc at the L.A. Italian eatery Pane e Vino. "They both have a lot going on," Doug Pitt said. "They haven't even been back to Springfield since November and they have no plans to return anytime soon."

Or, to quote a famous *Friends* line, was the couple "on a break"? At the end of April, Pitt headed to New York for a *Troy* publicity blitz. He cryptically admitted in a press room, "I'm not completely happy." The same night, Aniston was 3,000 miles away in L.A. to attend an event honoring her hairstylist Chris McMillan. The pattern repeated all week, as Pitt and Aniston made high-profile appearances, apart, on two coasts. (Coincidentally, the release of *Troy* and the airing of the last *Friends* episode occurred within a 24-hour span.) By May, the low murmur of marital problems turned into a five-alarm siren: West coast showbiz insiders swore that the couple were having problems and would announce their split by day's end.

It didn't happen. At the very time the news was supposed to break, Pitt talked about having kids on MTV's *Total Request Live*. And on *The Oprah Winfrey Show* that day (it was a taped episode), he compared Aniston to "the fire we all crowd around for warmth" and boasted, "she's really extraordinary ... she has taught me a lot."

On May 10, the couple dispelled all rumors by turning up together at the *Troy* premiere in NYC. As they patiently walked the red carpet line and signed autographs for their fans, Aniston rested her hand on his butt. He rubbed her upper back. At the after-party at Cipriani 42nd Street, Aniston sat on Pitt's lap as they chatted with Cindy Crawford and her husband, Rande Gerber. Later, they hit Bungalow 8, where they smoked cigarettes and chatted with friends. The next day, they took a private tour of The Whitney Museum — and watched the *Friends* finale together.

Still, their greatest performance was yet to come, as Aniston and Pitt jetted to France to promote *Troy* at the Cannes Film Festival. When they arrived to check into their seaside suite at the ultra posh Hotel du Cap Eden Roc on the French Riviera, their low-key intimacy charmed onlookers. They took each other's hands, walked slowly to check in without a bellboy, publicist, or an entourage.

The scene was considerably more frenzied at the Cannes *Troy* premiere. Aniston and Pitt, as glam-looking as ever, acted like the prom king and queen of the world as the paparazzi clamored for their attention. And, for once, the couple seemed to revel in the attention, as they beamed on the red carpet, whispered in each other's ear and shared private jokes. Afterward, they made a quick visit to the Picasso Museum in nearby Antibes, where they checked out works by the Russian abstract painter Nicholas de Stael. *Très* romantic, indeed.

The Brad and Jen show was in full-swing. Later that month, Pitt traveled to Tokyo to promote *Troy* and launch D.Side, his new jewelry collection (along with partners Guido and Giorgio Damiani). "My wife loves jewelry," Pitt explained at the event. "And I love my wife. She's always my inspiration. I started doing this because I wanted to make something very special for her."

Making good on her post-*Friends* promise to travel, Aniston headed to Rome on May 23 for a solid month. The occasion? Pitt and his pals (including George Clooney and Matt Damon) were filming *Ocean's Twelve*. Despite Pitt's workload, the trip was a true Roman holiday. The couple toured the Pantheon, the Coliseum, and the Fontana di Trevi — and shopped at the Prada boutique — all in a day. They also found time to eat at the historic, five-star Hotel de Russie.

The *amore* continued when Clooney opened up his twenty-five-room retreat in Lake Como for the couple and a few others, including Matt Damon and his steady, Luciana Barroso. On the itinerary: A boat ride (where Clooney's then-girlfriend, Lisa Snowdon, poured the wine), sunning, and a private pizza party. Onlookers said that Pitt and Aniston acted very tender with each other and kissed throughout their stay.

In July, Pitt took a break from filming in Rome to fly to London with Aniston for a weekend getaway. During their stay, they visited the tony auction houses Christie's and Sotheby's. Pitt and Aniston, along with some pals — including Claudia Schiffer — enjoyed a three-hour dinner at Fifteen, the restaurant owned by their favorite chef, Jamie Oliver. (After all the eating, a source at the Dorchester Hotel reported that Pitt asked to use the hotel gym at 3 A.M.)

The couple enjoyed another luxurious meal when they returned to Rome. As a surprise to Aniston, Pitt arranged a dinner with actor Dennis Haysbert, who played Julianne Moore's love interest in 2002's *Far From Heaven*, one of her favorite films. They dined for hours inside the Hotel Aleph, as the couple grilled Haysbert on his performance, his career, and discussed their own views on acting.

Unfortunately, the couple's golden summer

together had to come to an end. On July 21, the actress started work on her first post-*Friends* project, the *Graduate*-inspired comedy *Rumor Has It* which was costarring Mena Suvari and Kevin Costner. Pitt wrapped *Ocean's Twelve* and returned home shortly thereafter to start re-shoots on *Mr. and Mrs. Smith*. Still, he arrived just in time for the couple to spend their four-year anniversary together. Reportedly, Pitt's *Ocean's Twelve* love interest, Catherine Zeta-Jones, had advised him on what to get his wife. Get her a ruby, the actress allegedly said, explaining, "Call me old fashioned, but nothing says 'I love you' like a big, old rock."

They still looked liked newlyweds in late August when pal Scott Caan had a party celebrating an exhibition of his black and white photographs. At one point, reported an eyewitness, when Aniston stood and looked at a photograph, Pitt put his arms around her and gave her a big hug. "They didn't leave each other's sides the whole time," said a source. "She constantly had his hand on her waist."

On September 19, the couple arrived hand-in-hand to their fourth Emmy Awards. Aniston waved to the fans, while Pitt patiently stood off to the side and declined interviews.

"I'm off today," he explained, and cited fatigue after wrapping *Mr. and Mrs. Smith*. When asked if Aniston brought along any good-luck charms, she pointed to her husband. Apparently, he wasn't enough: She lost out to Sarah Jessica Parker, who had wrapped her own landmark comedy, *Sex and the City*, earlier in the year.

By fall, whether they realized it or not, Aniston and Pitt had begun to show the stripes of their relationship. Sources on the L.A. set of *Rumor Has It* reported that Pitt never dropped by to visit his wife. Soon, she would start filming her next movie, the thriller *Derailed*, costarring Clive Owen. Pitt immersed himself in politics. The devout Democrat wore a John Kerry T-shirt at an art event. A Kerry sign was on display in the driveway of their Beverly Hills mansion. On October 13, when he and Aniston hosted a star-studded, private screening of the documentary *Going Upriver: The Long War of John Kerry* at the Director's Guild of America, the couple worked the room separately. At one point, Pitt and Edward Norton talked in one corner on the patio, while a chain-smoking Aniston stayed on the other side with three girlfriends.

One week later, when Pitt presented *Going*

Upriver at his alma mater, the University of Missouri-Columbia, it was still obvious that his wife meant the most to him. During a post-screening dinner at Sophia's, one *Friends*-loving female fan approached the star and asked if he could autograph a photo of Aniston. Pitt not only happily obliged, he exclaimed, "She is amazing. Thank you so much for supporting her and supporting the show. It was a wonderful show and she's such a wonderful person. Thank you so much." Later, he talked with the stepdaughter of the county commissioner. When she told him that Jennifer Aniston was the most beautiful person in the world, he replied, "Thank you so much. I happen to agree with you. She's the nicest, sweetest person. She's really funny too! We have a fun time together."

Was it a case of wishful thinking? In November, Aniston was off to Chicago to start work on *Derailed*. A witness reported that she looked wet and miserable. When asked what it was like being separated from Pitt again, she answered, "It's awful!" They briefly reunited on November 25 for Thanksgiving: Aniston was spotted getting a haircut at Canale hair salon, while Pitt drove around town with his dad. The two had dinner at their home, then joined

LeBlanc and his family for a celebration. The next day, Pitt took his busy wife to LAX so she could resume filming.

It was reported they had a chilly goodbye.

CHAPTER 17

The Angelina Factor

Any story about Aniston and Pitt's relationship in 2004 would be remiss without proper mention of actress Angelina Jolie. After Nicole Kidman backed out of *Mrs. and Mrs. Smith*, Pitt tapped the sexy Oscar winner as his leading lady for the action romance. (In the film, Pitt and Jolie play married assassins hired to kill each other.) Nearly as soon as filming began, so did the rumors about an off-screen flirtation between the costars. Though everyone involved denied the allegations, the buzz played to Aniston's reported insecurities and possibly further crippled her already shaky marriage.

When filming began in L.A. in January 2004, Pitt and Jolie seemed to hit it off immediately. "Brad and Angelina have a genuine bond. They *get* each other," said a source from the set. When photos of the couple holding hands emerged, however, many wondered how deep the connection really was. Suspicions were further aroused when the couple once disappeared together in a trailer, only to emerge hours later. "They both went after each other," another insider, who worked closely with the stars, recalled. "It wasn't like she was just after him and seducing him. They wanted each other. It was pretty obvious."

After a shoot at the L.A. restaurant Cicada, the insider said the pair hit the deck of the hip Standard hotel and remained there until 5 A.M., long after the rest of the cast and crew had gone home. "The night at the Standard was nuts," recalled the source. "It was just the two of them in a roped off area on the rooftop, near the patch of grass. They wanted time alone and the staff made a booth space for them. I know for a fact they kissed."

Jolie and Pitt's reps strenuously denied the rumors of a fling. Said a Jolie insider, "Nothing improper happened. They were shooting at the hotel and there were production crews there, everyone there for the movie. It was not some date." Another source very close to the actress insisted, "She's never had any type of relationship with Brad outside of a professional one." Even a source close to the film's director, Doug Liman, said, "[Doug] never saw anything but friendship."

Naturally, the idea of two sultry superstars having an illicit romance sent the public and the media into a frenzy. And by summer, the whispers — whether true or not — had clearly taken a toll on Pitt. According to one Jolie insider, the actor had his people call her people to say: "Tell her to stay away from Brad. It's causing problems. Do not talk to the media about it." It seemed the actress respected his wishes, since a very close source confirmed that she had "distanced herself from Brad to avoid any suggestion of [an affair]."

As gorgeous and talented as Aniston is, it's a no-brainer as to why Jolie might have gotten under her skin. In a sense, she's every woman's worst nightmare: smart, beautiful, and undeniable sexy. In one of *Mr. and Mrs. Smith's* first scenes, Jolie's character goes undercover to play a prostitute who specializes in S&M. "She is supposed to strip down, tie this guy up and down and then kill him," said a source. The actress, who wielded a whip, was practically naked when she shot the scene. "Everyone's mouths dropped. It was like wow, 'look at her,'" she wasn't nervous or apprehensive in the slightest bit. Everyone, including Brad [who was not in the scene], was amazed at how good she was," added the source.

And then there's her little habit of hooking up with her costars. In 1996, she married British actor Jonny Lee Miller, who starred opposite her in the film *Hackers*. At the wedding, the actress wore leather pants and a white T-shirt on which she had scrawled Miller's name in her own blood. They split the following year. "We were simply too young," she said. In hindsight, it was a move the actress regretted. "Divorcing Jonny was probably the dumbest thing I've ever done," she confessed. (In February 2004, it seemed as if the couple might reunite when they were spotted kissing at Shamrock Social Club in West Hollywood; afterward she spent $150 on a "Know Your Rights" tattoo between her shoulder blades.) She later admitted that she had an affair with her *Foxfire* costar Jenny Simizu during the marriage.

In spring 1998, Jolie met Billy Bob Thornton on the set of the comedy *Pushing Tin*. At the time, he was engaged to actress Laura Dern, but two years later he decided Jolie was The One. "I left our home to work on a movie," said Dern, "and while I was away my boyfriend got married, and I've never heard from him again."

In May, he and Jolie said "I do" at the Little Church of the West Wedding Chapel in Las Vegas. "We were like kids in high school," she said of the relationship. "We were both crazy happy to have found a friend." Crazy was right: Over the course of their marriage, the couple wore vials of each other's blood around their necks and told a reporter on the red carpet of the 2000 MTV Movie Awards that they had just had sex in their limo; Thornton was rumored to have occasionally worn his wife's underwear.

But it wasn't meant to be. Four months after Jolie adopted seven-month-old Cambodian orphan Maddox in March 2002, she filed for divorce from Thornton. ("It's clear that our priorities shifted overnight," said Jolie, who serves as a Goodwill Ambassador for the United Nations High Commissioner for Refugees). The nail in the coffin came on her twenty-seventh birthday, when she insisted on taking a flying lesson instead of sharing the time with her hubby. "They moved into hotels and stopped talking. It was very immature," said a source. But the actor still sounded heartbroken over his split when he lamented in 2003, "I will always love her dearly."

The busy single mom made time for romance by adopting a very wild, unorthodox love life. "I've decided to get closer to men who were already very close friends of mine... I have lovers," she proclaimed in 2004. Though she didn't cop to one-night stands, she admitted, "meeting a man in a hotel room for a few hours... and then not seeing that man again for a few months is what I can handle now."

Jolie's public declaration shed new light on her relationships with her sexy male costars. During the summer of 2003, for instance, she was photographed kissing her *Taking Lives* costar Ethan Hawke in a trailer on the Montreal set (at the time, he and wife Uma Thurman, were estranged). "Ethan is a wonderful, good man, and a great father," she said. Hawke was equally adulatory toward Jolie when he remarked in March 2004, "Every now and then, God gets it exactly right."

Meanwhile, according to a source, in November 2003, she and her *Alexander* onscreen husband, Val Kilmer, met several times in a bar inside the Raffles L'Ermitage Beverly Hills hotel. There, he allegedly told a waitress he'd like "Angelina Jolie on a plate." The actress denied it: "We [worked] together, but we're not anything else."

And then there was the rendezvous with her *Alexander* son, Colin Farrell. First, the costars were spotted drinking, dancing, and cozying up to each other at London hot spots like the Langham Hilton bar, Annabel's, and the club Elysium. "They spent a lot of time giggling," said an eyewitness. In late December

2003, Jolie and Farrell (with Maddox in tow), spent the Christmas holidays together in Egypt, where the threesome visited the pyramids in Giza and embarked on camel rides. Clearly, the two had much in common — ranging from their wild-child lifestyles, to their devotion to their children (Farrell's son James was born months before production started). But neither of the outspoken parties ever confirmed a hookup. "He's just a wonderful and great guy," she said in 2004.

Despite suggestions to the contrary, sources close to Pitt and Jolie insisted that the pair were platonic — after all, it's not uncommon for costars to spend quality time together during shoots. "They often spend a huge amount of time together and very strong bonds form," explained Los Angeles-based acting coach Jill Place. "When you are on a project, your cast mates become like your family. In most cases, spouses are not around much and that makes it even easier for actors to get attached to their costars."

Things can become even more complicated when the script calls for romance. "Actors bring part of themselves to every role, so when they play characters in love, it sometimes carries over after cameras stop rolling," she explained. Even when emotions aren't involved, flirtatious behavior between costars isn't frowned upon. "Everything is appropriate when you are on set," she says. "Bottom line is that actors have to create a reality."

They certainly had plenty of conversation topics to keep them occupied — most notably Jolie's role as a Goodwill Ambassador. The actress, who donates a large percentage of her earnings to humanitarian aid efforts, is an advocate for issues such as world hunger (she took the flying lessons in hope that one day she might be able to deliver food to needy people) and the removal of land mines. In November, Pitt joined the landmine crusade. "He is an incredibly caring person and he wants to give something back," said Mike Kendrick of Mineseekers charity group.

Indeed, Pitt never denied his admiration for his *Mr. and Mrs. Smith* costar. "I tell you, I've never seen someone so misperceived as Jolie," Pitt told reporters while promoting *Troy*. "Because she's a really decent human being, and very dedicated with her U.N. work, and very dedicated to her child. It's a daily thing for her. I was really surprised to see, I mean, I even had my own...not feeling, but just the perception that's out there. She's really surprisingly level-headed and bright and incredibly decent." She's also 180-degrees different than the cool, introverted Aniston. "Angelina is like a breath of fresh air," said a source. "He feels free with her and he loves the kid and thinks she's a great mom and doesn't take herself too seriously."

The cast and crew took a three-month hiatus from *Mr. and Mrs. Smith* while Pitt shot *Ocean's Twelve*. But when the production reconvened in August, at the very least, it was obvious that the stars had forged a close friendship. By late October 2004, when the film's locale moved to Amalfi, Italy, Pitt and Jolie made of the most of their four days in each other's company. "They were together all the time," recalled a source at the Hotel Santa Caterina, where they both stayed. Though Pitt's room was in the main house, the pair was often spotted in the hotel's lush gardens, where Jolie's honeymoon suite was situated. "When they ordered food, they'd have room service on the terrace of Angelina's suite." Other times, added the insider, "They were both playing with her little boy [Maddox] and running around, chasing each other and laughing together all day long. Brad and the boy were climbing trees and beautiful Angelina was smiling and clapping."

Eyewitnesses also noticed the chemistry when the couple was at work in nearby Ravello. "Angelina was the biggest flirt! Every time she would walk past Brad she would purposely brush her shoulders up against him," said a witness. "She was always touching him. They were always near each other when they weren't filming. She had that sultry look all the time. She would lean into him and look at him!" Pitt was responsive to the attention, said the onlooker. "They were joking around together. He definitely wasn't ignoring her. He would talk to her and laugh. They clearly got along quite well. If I didn't know he was married to Jennifer Aniston, I would have thought they were a couple."

So what affect did the Angelina factor ultimately have on Aniston and Pitt's union? "The marriage was already starting to loosen around then [the time of *Mr. and Mrs. Smith*] and it certainly didn't make things better," said an insider. Indeed a set source recalled that the actor's behavior hinted at the changes in his personal life. "The way Brad interacted with Angelina was not at all the way a married man would act with another woman," said the source. "Neither of them cheated on each other," added an insider. "They were moving in different directions." In fact, at a bash at NYC's Maritime hotel in May, Pitt was overheard commenting on an attractive female guest. "Someone made an indirect reference to Aniston and he said [something to the likes of], 'the grass is always greener.'"

The Jolie buzz — however much it was denied — clearly troubled Aniston. "Jennifer saw the pictures [of Pitt and Jolie] and heard some things and it made her insecure," revealed a source. It also couldn't have helped that Pitt bonded with little Maddox, just as he and his wife were battling over when to start a family. "He loves Maddox. It was part of the attraction [to her]," said a source. And he loved to illustrate his affection for the toddler: On set one day, "Brad got up and started imitating Maddox's walk, swaying and teetering on the grass. It was very funny! Angelina was laughing."

Jolie, for her part, has maintained her innocence. In the November 2004 issue of *Allure* she said, "I wouldn't sleep with a married man. I have enough lovers. I don't need Brad."

CHAPTER 18

A Long December

As 2004 was winding down, so was the couple's relationship. At the beginning of December, they were separated by more than 6,000 miles, with Aniston on the London set of *Derailed* and Pitt in the States, kicking off his whirlwind promotional blitz for *Ocean's Twelve*. Pitt generally seemed jovial and relaxed during this period, while Aniston's mood was mixed, according to set sources. Breakup buzz then hit a fever pitch when Pitt left his wife in London, and the actress was then reportedly spotted without her wedding ring. The sightings proved false, but the damage, perhaps, was already done.

Still, on December 2, it seemed the couple's future was solid. The *Ocean's Twelve* cast made their first major appearance in a taped interview with Diane Sawyer on ABC's *Primetime Live*. The group had gathered at the Palm Springs home of the film's producer, Jerry Weintraub, for a weekend of golfing and relaxing. (Spouses were welcome, but only Catherine Zeta Jones's husband Michael Douglas made the trip.) With buddies George Clooney, Matt Damon, and Pitt in the same room, viewers were guaranteed a few laughs — and got them — but the joking turned bittersweet when Sawyer asked each cast member where they hoped to see themselves in three years. "God, I'm going to say it," Pitt began, becoming visibly emotional and briefly covering his eyes. "Kids. Family. I'm thinking family. Yeah. I got family on the mind." Earlier, Sawyer referred to comments he had made in the past about wanting daughters. "Yeah," he confirmed. "Jen and I, we're working something out. [Little girls], they crush me. They break my heart ... You know, I'm going to get all boys just because of it ... Listen, I'll take them all at this point. I'll take them all." Though he had been vocal about wanting kids before, Pitt's yearning seemed stronger than ever.

Meanwhile, babies seemed to be the *furthest* thing from Aniston's mind as she worked and played in London. While her husband's heartache was being broadcast at home, she took in a screening of *Closer* (which starred her *Derailed* costar Clive Owen) with some coworkers. Despite the cold weather that caused Aniston to cuddle up to a pal and pull her fur-trimmed coat tighter, she looked quite content as she left the theater. "Jennifer was having a great night," reported an onlooker. "She was really chatting and joking with her group of friends." It was a much-needed time-out for the actress, who had been working long hours ever since she arrived in town. "The film's got some pretty heavy scenes in it too," revealed a set source about Aniston's work. "She's raped by Vincent Cassell's character which has been really hard and dark to film, so it's not surprising she's been pretty wiped out when they call it a day."

The group's first stop after the movie was the members-only Century Club, where the *Derailed* cast and crew were gathered. Once inside, Aniston spent time chatting with Owen. "Clive and Jennifer were in their own private conversation for quite a long time and seemed to be talking about something very intensely," reported an eyewitness. "Then she broke off from talking just to him and talked to the group as a whole." Though she was far from the Hollywood rumor mill, she couldn't escape the baby buzz. According to the source, a guest "congratulated her on being pregnant. But Jennifer said, 'I'm not pregnant. It's just one of those stories that's going around.' Then she nodded toward her champagne glass to prove it." (That night, however, some keen observers noted she wasn't spotted smoking.)

Later on, she and about seven pals headed to a bash at Kabaret's Prophecy, where they drank at least five bottles of Cristal champagne before heading home at 5 A.M. (Jude Law's fiancée, Sienna Miller, was also at the club that night.) Said a source, "Jennifer was a very generous tipper. She left the £80 'change' at each throw so she racked up about £3600 worth of bar bill." Not even the bathroom attendant was stiffed! "Jennifer was great, she tipped big," said the ladies lounge worker. "She was one of the biggest hits I've ever got." It wasn't only Aniston's generosity that impressed the locals, but also her laid-back attitude. The previous evening, she and coworkers had stopped into Lonsdale pub in the Notting Hill section of the city and made no effort to hide from the public. "You'd imagine Jennifer would want to sit in a corner and be discrete," noted a manager at the bar, "but she was sat on a barstool laughing and chatting very animatedly. She was totally unstarry, very down to earth."

Though she was having a good time that evening, a source on the London set suspected something was weighing on the actress.

"There was a hint of melancholy about Jennifer," said the insider. "At the time, most of us who commented on it blamed it on the long hours and the stressful scenes, but in retrospect it could very easily have been her marriage break-up." Another source felt that over the course of filming, the actress pulled back and became more serious. "She also wore sunglasses between scenes for a few days for the first time, which made it harder to judge her mood," observed the source. But being a consummate professional, she never cried in public or discussed any personal issues. Still, recalled the first insider, "it was quite obvious there was something wrong although she never actually addressed the issue."

On December 4, Pitt and pal Catherine Keener hit a birthday party for his *Ocean's Twelve* costar Don Cheadle; afterward, they moved on to Keener's sister's own bash. On December 8, a solo Pitt walked the red carpet at the premiere of *Ocean's Twelve* in L.A. Just two days later, he and the gang were in Rome, the first stop on their European press tour — which would eventually lead him to London and Aniston. By all accounts, the actor was in good spirits throughout the trip. On Saturday, December 11, Pitt and a group that included

Weintraub had an intimate dinner at Dal Bolognese, a restaurant that became a favorite of the cast's when they filmed in the city just months before. "Brad seemed very relaxed and very happy," said an onlooker. "They were having fun." The Paris premiere followed before Pitt jetted to Berlin. During a press conference with the German media, he seemed eager to reunite with Aniston. "I'm looking forward to spending Christmas with my wife," he said. "We both worked really hard this year and now want to ease off." Despite these statements, at least one witness saw hidden meaning in the actor's body language, saying, "When he said this, it was strange, 'cause he glanced away for a second and looked sad."

Back in England, some suspected Aniston was preparing to greet her husband with a sexy surprise. An eyewitness revealed that on December 15, the actress scooped up lacy lingerie and sex toys at London's Myla boutique, a high-end shop known for their vibrators that double as works of art. "She said she really loved the store and was very impressed with the range of underwear it sold," the source reported. Her favorites: 1/4 cup bras that give lift but without covering the nipple area, and a plunge bra that Christina Aguilera wore in one of her videos. "After she had looked through the lingerie section she went straight to where the sex toys were and bought two of them," said the source. "One of them was a steel cylindrical tube and the other was a flat thing that vibrates." Upon learning the intimate details of this shopping spree, Aniston's representative was quick to claim the star "never stepped foot in the store."

Wherever Jennifer had actually been, the stage was set for the couple to spend some quality time together, with the highlight being Pitt's birthday on December 18. According to sources, Aniston was going to take her husband to London's Camden Market and Portobello Road Market. For the evening celebration, she had reportedly looked into hosting a birthday party at in the VIP room at The Penthouse, a swank restaurant and club. "Some of her people came down and had a look at the area and seemed to really like it and were going on about how it would be a great place for a party because the views were so lovely and Brad loves the architecture," revealed a Penthouse insider. "But we never actually got contacted for a booking and we were told in the end that they were both having to go back to L.A. to celebrate so they wouldn't need it."

Pitt and Aniston's reps denied there were ever any plans to go to The Penthouse, but that does not explain what happened in the days to come. Originally, the stars were scheduled to return to L.A. together on December 23, but the *Derailed* production scheduled was tightened and the wrap date moved up. On December 16, the day Pitt arrived in London, Aniston reported to work as usual. Pitt was scheduled to attend an *Ocean's Twelve* press conference at Claridge's Hotel, but an early morning fire in the building prevented it from taking place at all. (The actor, who was staying with his wife at the Dorchester hotel, was not on the premises at the time of the fire.)

That evening, the couple attended a party at a home in Notting Hill. "Brad went to the party from the Dorchester and Jennifer went to the party straight from the film studios," said a source. When they returned to their hotel at 2 A.M., "They seemed happy and were smiling as they went up to their suite. There didn't seem to be any animosity between then at all. They certainly didn't seem like a couple on the edge of a break-up." In fact, the next day they even had reservations to dine with pals at one of their favorite restaurants, La Famiglia in Chelsea. At the last minute, the reservation was changed. Pitt was heading to Japan for more promotional work, said a restaurant staffer. At noon on December 17, the actor — acting as pleasant as ever, according to hotel staffers — hopped into a blacked-out SUV and was driven to Luton airport where a private jet was awaiting. The destination: not Japan, but L.A.

At the same time, a British newspaper was reporting that Aniston had flown back home because of the death of a friend, and that Pitt had canceled his plans to be by her side. A source later confirmed that Aniston's therapist had died, but the actress did not leave town that day. Instead, she and eight friends celebrated the end of the *Derailed* shoot with dinner at La Famiglia. "She was laughing with her friends and having fun," said Alvaro, the maître'd. She told me she was flying back to Los Angeles and was excited about going home." But with one more day of work, she didn't make it there in time for Pitt's forty-first birthday. In a sharp contrast to celebrations of years past, Pitt was spotted alone that afternoon, riding his Ducati motorcycle outside their Beverly Hills home.

With two bottles of Fiji water in hand, Jennifer Aniston checked out of the Dorchester hotel on December 19, and took off for Heathrow airport and her flight home. "She looked really miserable as she left the hotel," said an eyewitness. "She's usually fairly resigned to being photographed, but she was in a really bad mood and did everything she could to hide her face and get out of the photographs." As she walked out, the star played with her wedding ring. "She was either taking it off or putting it on," said the onlooker. By the time she got into the car she had opted to keep it on." (It was reported that she wasn't wearing the white-gold ring at all, but subsequent photos showed it was just not visible in many photos.) She arrived at LAX looking somber and with her hands clenched, but her publicist later shot down talk that the marriage was, indeed, in trouble. "They are together and are looking forward to enjoying the holidays with each other," he announced. "There is no split. They are fine."

CHAPTER 19

Their Final Days

It made perfect sense. After crisscrossing the globe for the majority of 2004, Aniston and Pitt decided to take a relaxing and romantic time-out by spending a week in the tropical Caribbean island of Anguilla. Best of all, their friends Courteney Cox and David Arquette (and their seven-month-old daughter, Coco) were along for the ride. Of course, as it turned out, there was deep trouble in paradise. By the time they left the island on January 8, 2005, the marriage was over.

★ ★ ★

The trip started off pleasantly enough. The foursome (along with non-celeb pals John and Corey Finch) flew on a private jet from LAX to Anguilla two days after Christmas. Their final destination: The Exclusivity Villa at Captain's Bay, a swank 15,000-square-foot mansion with five bedrooms, ocean views, flat-screen TVs, and a full-time chef. The rate: $20,000 a week. The resort was rumored to be owned by the family of none other than Senator John Kerry.

The group embraced their surroundings. On December 30, they tried to reserve a beach day at the resort Cap Juluca — but couldn't because fellow VIP P. Diddy already had booked the slot. As an alternative, Courteney, David, and Coco tanned and played in the water, while the Pitts remained secluded until dinner.

The party continued on New Year's Eve. At 9 P.M., the foursome hit Cap Juluca's casual restaurant, George's, for a $150-a-pop buffet, where they joined Uma Thurman and her boyfriend, Andre Balazs, and Liam Neeson and his wife, actress Natasha Richardson. "They ate like champs," said an onlooker, who noted that both gals went back for thirds of dishes like ribs, fish, and mashed potatoes. Nothing seemed amiss, especially when Pitt put on a plastic New Year's top hat and rang a noisemaker. "There was a lot of joking and laughing — They were taking pictures. It was more like a group of friends hanging out — not a last dinner type of thing." Though one onlooker noted, "Brad seemed in a much better mood than Jen. And there was not much interaction between them. Jennifer was talking more to Courteney than to her husband. David and Brad were doing the guy thing."

Just before midnight, the men returned to the villa with a bottle of red wine. The girls followed shortly thereafter, and at midnight, the foursome rang in the year 2005 in private. "They're great together," said a source of the foursome. "You have to be to spend that much time together on vacation."

The group didn't emerge until they were ferried by boat to the small island of Scilly Cay on January 2, where they devoured a two-hour-plus lunch. And they were still in good spirits: Pitt stood and bopped to the music of Happy Hits, a local acoustic band, then grabbed his wife from behind and hugged her. Aniston put her arm around him. Though their days together as an official couple were numbered, they gave no indication of it. "They were all over each other like a rash," said one native. "They had their paws all over each other and they were kissing the whole time." Upon their return, Pitt drove his scooter back to their villa alone while the others rode in a minivan.

The next day, the group checked out of the Exclusivity Villa and moved into the $35,000 a week Brazillian Emerald Villa — a five-bedroom, private beachfront mansion with its own pool, hot tub, fitness center, home theater, and butler — at the fabulously posh Altamer resort (located near the island's southwest tip). Immediately, a shirtless Pitt took advantage of his surroundings and played basketball on the private court.

But despite the happy front, the couple privately broke the news to close friends and family. On January 4, Pitt traveled solo to Miami, where he met up with his dad, his uncle, his brother, and several friends to watch the FedEx Orange Bowl championship college football game from a VIP suite. When Pitt awoke around seven the next morning at the Ritz-Carlton, Key Biscayne, he joined his uncle on the terrace to drink coffee and talk — and break the news of the impending split. "They were in deep conversation for nearly an hour," says an onlooker. "Brad had large bags under his eyes."

Pitt rarely ventured out of his suite during his less-than-24-hour stay in Key Biscayne (his suite, ironically, overlooked the hotel's child daycare center). "He did not go to the restaurants, spa, beach or pool," said a hotel source. "He was very quiet, just relaxed in this suite. He was super charming, but definitely wanted to be left alone." Later that day, he traveled via private plane back to the island to rejoin his group. He was back by dinnertime.

Aniston and Pitt's last official day as a couple was perhaps the most emotional in their seven-year relationship. First, the duo, along with the Cox and Arquette, enjoyed a casual late-afternoon lunch at eatery Trattoria Tramonto. Said an onlooker, "You could hear the pitch rise in the restaurant when they walked in, but they looked very relaxed." And, yes, affectionate. "They were so sweet! He was saying 'Jen, dear' to her," recalled the source, adding that they were both wearing their wedding rings.

Then, the walk into the sunset: Shortly after 5 P.M., Pitt and Jennifer clung to each other as they strolled down the beach to their villa. With one arm draped around his wife's shoulder, Pitt kissed her on her head and twice on her lips during the short outing. When they reached the villa, Aniston stopped to look at some shells in the sand and Pitt never took his eyes off her. "They weren't even looking where they were walking," said one eyewitness. "They were just looking at each other the whole time. They looked so happy." As much as the thought makes their fans cringe, was it another performance by two of Hollywood's most popular actors?

On January 7, the couple spent the day separated (physically, that is). Aniston, in a bikini top and denim shorts, accompanied by Cox and Finch, spent most of the day on the beach at their villa, where Aniston cooed over the adorable baby Coco; Pitt and Arquette took off for an afternoon snorkeling excursion.

By day's end, the couple's reps released the official statement that Aniston and Pitt had decided to split. Perhaps nobody was more shocked than the Anguilla locals, who had seen the couple act like newlyweds for the past week. "I can't believe this!" said a bartender at Cap Juluca. "They came here three nights in a row and seemed happy. They seemed like just another couple." Said another, "It makes no sense. I've seen them around all week, and if that isn't love, I don't know what is. They're still calling each other 'honey.' They're still kissing…." And an employee of the Caribbean Tourist Board in Anguilla remarked, "The news of Hollywood's golden couple splitting up came as a deep surprise to those of us who saw them frolic on the beach. I guess it reinforces their abilities as actors."

Others were less blown away by the news. "They weren't cold to each other, but they weren't hot like Uma and Andre either," said one onlooker. Another witness was blunt: "Jen was giving the 'get off me' look." Others duly noted that Pitt did his best to maintain a calming front for his emotional wife. "Brad kept putting his arms around her and making sure she was OK," said a Scilly Cay waitress. "He was looking after Jennifer and that was his main concern." Said another, "He was way more into her than she was into him." The restaurant manager at Altamer added, "He kept kissing her. He kissed her all the time."

But one staffer, who revealed that the couple informed a few of the hotel's key employees of the bad news earlier in the week, was optimistic: "He said the split was for a little while," said the source, who added that the couple planned to return to the island later in the year. "They're not completely broken up."

On January 8, with the world reeling from the shocking news, Aniston and Pitt added a final — and perplexing — chapter to their bittersweet getaway. At 10 A.M., the couple, still wearing their wedding rings, held hands and intertwined their arms, when they departed Anguilla via Summertime, a chartered boat that was used by Beyoncé Knowles and her boyfriend, Jay-Z, the week before. They sailed to nearby island St. Maarten, where the couple's private plane took them back to the Van Nuys airport in L.A.

The vacation was over. The couple arrived in L.A., where, perhaps aptly, pouring rain filled the sky. Not surprisingly, one of the world's most famous couples was greeted by a horde of photographers. Aniston and Pitt (who donned sunglasses) didn't say a word and darted to their waiting SUV-style limousine. While in the backseat, they sat apart, stared straight ahead and hardly interacted. Their presence in the SUV attracted such a media entourage, a police SUV had to escort them en route to Beverly Hills. Finally, the pair reached the gates of their beloved mansion and entered their abode unscathed.

Their emotional scars cut far deeper.

Days after the 189 was announced, it still remained a mystery as to why a couple would spend their last days together on a carefree vacation. Were they getting away from their problems — or gearing up for the end? Most likely, a little bit of both. "It may have been a last-ditch effort on the part of one to change the other's mind," says Dr. Lieberman. On an island far away from the rest of the world, they could indulge the fantasy that "somehow the other would see things their way, give it one last try," she says. And, staying true to their claim that the split was amicable, they may have wanted a sweet goodbye. "It's not like they hate each other," says Lieberman. "They still love spending time together even if there's a longing in each of them, wishing that things were different."

The serene setting also provided an opportunity for the Pitts to break the news to their best friends — who were heartbroken by the news. "Jennifer told Courteney they had something to talk about, but she didn't think it was this," said a source close to Cox and Arquette. "They sat them down, and, of course, David and Courteney were upset but supportive. Brad and Jennifer said they would continue to be friends and that everything had just become too much. David and Courteney understood, but they were still surprised it had come down to [a split]." Another source speculated that witnessing Cox and Arquette's devotion to one another was "a real eye-opener" for Pitt and Aniston.

And despite the melancholy mood of the trip, the group ended up making the most of their time together. "They all wanted to still have a great time and be together as couples even through Brad and Jen were there trying things out as friends," said the source. "Basically, the trip was a way for them all to talk about everything and be comfortable in the decision before it was announced."

CHAPTER 20

What's Next?

Between the tsunami devastation, serious flooding on the West Coast, the historic Palestinian elections, and the war in Iraq, there was no shortage of headlines on January 10, 2004. Still, no journalist could turn away from the biggest celebrity break-up of the century. "I know there's a lot of news, but I think everybody was really sad to hear [that] Jennifer Aniston and Brad Pitt were calling it quits," a visibly disappointed Katie Couric said at the start of the *Today* show broadcast. "They seemed so happy and seemed so nice."

In Hollywood, The Split was the talk of the town, as countless celebrities weighed in with their reactions. "I'm shocked," said close friend and ex-costar Matt LeBlanc at the January 9 People's Choice Awards, where Pitt — a winner for Favorite Leading Man — was a no-show. Seconded an empathetic Jennifer Garner, "One thing I've learned is that the only two people who know what is going on in a relationship are the people who are in it. I just feel for both of them."

Their peers were still shocked and saddened one week later at the 62nd Annual Golden Globe Awards (where, two years earlier, a victorious Aniston neglected to thank her husband). "I was surprised," said actress Mena Suvari, who spent considerable time with Aniston just months earlier on the set of *Rumor Has It*. "I think it's unfortunate when any marriage ends. I just wish them all the best for the future." *The Sopranos'* actress Jamie-Lynn Discala, who wed her manager, A. J. Discala, in 2003, agreed. "All I can say is, knowing the effort and care you put into a marriage, it's hard when the relationship isn't working. They are two grown people and obviously two lovely people and I wish the best for them."

And, inevitably, the breakup blitz provided the perfect fodder for comics. "I think once you have been Achilles, you are vulnerable," joked Robin Williams, in reference to Pitt's *Troy*. "Life is tough. He is a stud muffin. Jennifer hasn't called. I called her. 'Would you like an older hairy man?' It is quite the simian experience." Late-night talk-show host Jimmy Kimmel chimed in, "I lay awake nights thinking about it. I know she's back with Ross now." And, during one *Saturday Night Live* sketch on January 15 — nearly a year-to-the-day after Aniston sported that "I Love Brad Pitt" T-shirt and joked about her pressure to procreate on the show — two burly truck drivers (one played by host Topher Grace) cried out in anguish over the bad news.

But to the devastated Pitt and Aniston family members, the grieving was all too real — and hardly a laughing matter. "They're both family — Brad *and* Jen," said an emotional Doug Pitt. "We'll be supportive of both of them, as much as we can." Meanwhile, Aniston's upset dad, John, told a source, "It was Brad who instigated the split." As for her estranged mom, Nancy, who never met her son-in-law but was still surprised by the news, she simply stated, "I do not want to make any comment about my daughter, thank you."

Ironically, it seemed like Pitt and Aniston were the ones least affected by the announcement. Instead of hiding out inside their estates, the couple took a business-as-usual attitude as they went on — albeit with their separate lives.

On January 11, Aniston began her first day filming the aptly titled dramedy, *Friends with Money*. Ironically, the actress portrays Joan, the lone single woman among three close girlfriends, played by Aniston's real-life (and married) pals Catherine Keener, Frances McDormand, and Joan Cusack. Working behind-the-scenes as one of the first camera operators was Danny Moder, the husband of Julia Roberts, who was Pitt's costar in *The Mexican*, *Ocean's Eleven*, and *Ocean's Twelve*.

The actress arrived to the set — a massive ballroom inside the beachside Casa Del Mar Hotel in Santa Monica — at 10:30 AM. She wore torn jeans, a black shirt, and her wedding ring. In a case of bad timing, her first scene required her to play a wedding guest. During a short rehearsal scene, according to a source, Aniston seemed happy and focused as she discussed the scene with writer-director Nicole Holofcener and gave input. "She walked in to the ballroom like it was a normal work day," said the source. "You would never guess that she had just separated. She seemed really excited and happy about being there."

In fact, Aniston was even offered to have the wedding scene postponed by the producer, but "she seemed eager to stick to the shooting schedule." After her day's work at 9 P.M., Aniston was whisked off to the luxurious Shutters On The Beach, where she spent the night. The next morning, she promptly arrived at 8

A.M. to the movie set, which had changed locales to the Santa Monica Farmer's Market, followed by the James Beach Café in Venice. She still wore the ring.

Once again, Pitt was a trans-Atlantic flight away. On January 13, he and *Ocean's Twelve* cast mates Clooney and Damon traveled to Tokyo for the film's press conference and premiere. In an attempt to make the trip as painless as possible, all non-Japanese reporters were banned from the news conference, and, per Pitt's reps, local press were required to sign a contract forbidding them from asking any personal questions. It was easier said than done: As the A-list hunks disembarked from their flight at Narita International Airport, fans and media swarmed the scene. And when one reporter reportedly asked Pitt about the breakup, Clooney intervened and scolded, "Shame on you."

Otherwise, their twenty-four hours in Japan went like clockwork. During their one-hour conference, the stars made good on their trademark boys-will-be-boys banter. "Brad had fun joking with George and Matt," said one eyewitness. During one interview — which Pitt did not partake in — Clooney sarcastically replied to a question about Pitt, "I don't know, I haven't read the paper, but I've heard he's pulled some other publicity stunts in the last couple of days…" Damon then quipped, "He's desperate!"

The what-me-worry attitude continued later that night when Pitt and his pals arrived to the premiere at Roppongi Hills. "He was very friendly," said one fan, who got Pitt's autograph on the red carpet. And when Pitt took the stage before the film started, he surprised fans by pulling his hands from his coat pocket, which revealed his wedding ring. "It's like he was advertising that he still wore it," added the fan. Post-screening, the gang enjoyed a private dinner at An Roppongi Hills, an authentic Japanese restaurant. Clooney, Damon, and Pitt were on a flight back home to Los Angeles by 11:30 P.M.

The threesome publicly reunited in L.A. on January 15, but for a much less-celebratory reason: They were among dozens of stars participating in an NBC's *Tsunami Aid: A Concert of Hope* telethon for the South Asia relief effort, which was organized by Clooney. Pitt did not speak on camera, and instead opted to man a phone line. "No one talked about Jen or the breakup," said an on-set source. "Everyone just focused on doing the work." His presence prompted unofficial host Jay Leno to crack to the prospective female viewers, "And girls... Brad Pitt's here also."

Judging by the couple's behavior in the aftermath of the announcement, it was clear that the Aniston and Pitt separation was an amicable one. Still, as two powerful and successful celebrities who reportedly did *not* sign a prenuptial agreement, the couple faced tough decisions about their future —especially if the separation led to divorce.

Simply put, the financial facts of two powerful celebrities can't be ignored. Aniston, who commanded $5 million for the hit *Along Came Polly*, had reportedly upped her asking price to $7 million a film. But that was pocket change compared to Aniston's *Friends* fortune. According to *Forbes*, the actress — ranked No. 17 on the magazine's 2004 list of the world's 100 most powerful celebrities — took home nearly $20 million for the final season of *Friends* and will earn at least $8 million a year from royalties of *Friends* reruns. In total, she's estimated to be worth $75 million. And Pitt? Ranked No. 36 on the *Forbes* list, the actor earns about $17.5 per film, including *Mr. and Mrs. Smith*. His estimated net worth: $100 million.

But their fortunes might work to their advantage, according to family attorney Lynn Soodik (who represented Meg Ryan in her 2001 divorce from Dennis Quaid). She said, "they're practically equal money earners. And with no kids, no spousal-support or child support issues, there is simply nothing to figh about."

Insiders suggest that, career-wise, it's Aniston who may have the edge moving forward. "The breakup could be her big break," said movie columnist Martin Grove. "It takes her to a new level, creates enormous global media interest in her and creates worldwide fascination with her from moviegoers. It translates into making her a bankable star." But Gitesh Pandya, editor of boxofficeguru.com countered, "Brad Pitt is in the better position. He remains one of the world's most popular draws."

Inevitably, the biggest question of all comes up — could Aniston and Pitt reconcile their differences and live happily ever after? "They are not getting divorced yet," one source close to the pair explained. "This is just to see if things would be better if they're not together. They're just allowing the relationship time to breathe." Another pal has insisted, "They aren't talking divorce." And it can't hurt to consider Aniston's recent meditation on her marriage: "Once, when Brad and I were driving we saw the sweetest thing: an elderly couple in a Toyota Corolla. They were both older than time, and I don't know how they were even driving. Her little hands were shaking on the steering wheel. Then he just reached over and touched her hand. It was a moment that seemed to say, I've loved you for 70,000 years, and I still do.' I hope that's Brad and me someday."

But for now, the couple remains at peace with the decision, as they work through the most complicated chapter in their lives. "Jennifer has known the marriage wasn't working for awhile, so it's really not that big of a deal," said a source close to the Aniston. "They have basically been living as friends before, so it's life as usual for her. The only difference is now the rest of the world knows." And on January 13, Pitt's pal Clooney reassured the public, "Brad's doing great. I think he's holding up well. They are both holding up well. The trick now is, he's trying to continue with his life as normal as possible."

It's too soon to say if their sorrowful fans will recover with such optimism. But regardless of what the future holds for Hollywood's Golden Couple, one thing is clear: Whether they're together or apart, Jennifer Aniston and Brad Pitt will always be loved.

About the Authors

MARA REINSTEIN is a senior writer at *Us Weekly*, where she has written countless news stories about Brad Pitt and Jennifer Aniston (not to mention dozens of *Friends* features). Before joining the staff in July 2002, she was an entertainment staff writer at *Teen People*. She has also worked at *Broadcasting & Cable* magazine and *McCall's*.

JOEY BARTOLOMEO is a senior writer at *Us Weekly*, where she has been chronicling the lives of Brad Pitt and Jennifer Aniston, Britney Spears, Justin Timberlake, Cameron Diaz, Jennifer Lopez, and others since 2000. Previously, she was a writer and editor at *Allure*, *Harper's Bazaar*, and *Conde Nast Women's Sport & Fitness*.